The Millionaire in the Pew

A manual on major and deferred gift fundraising *for* clergy and religious leaders

By Russell L. Wilson, M.Div.

WestBow Press books may be ordered through booksellers or by contacting:

WestBow Press
A Division of Thomas Nelson
1663 Liberty Drive
Bloomington, IN 47403
www.westbowpress.com
1-(866) 928-1240

ISBN: 978-1-4497-3388-9 (sc)
ISBN: 978-1-4497-3390-2 (e)

Library of Congress Control Number: 2011962533

Printed in the United States of America

WestBow Press rev. date: 01/12/2012

PREFACE

Many books have been written about the subject of stewardship for pastors and church leaders. Some have been written about fundraising, primarily for professionals in that field. This book skillfully bridges the gap between stewardship and fundraising and designs a ministry of fundraising for clergy and religious leaders. The book emerges at a critical time in the life of the Church.

In normal economic times, most churches could put additional contributions to good use. However, it is painfully obvious that in this time of recession, many churches are struggling to meet their budgets. Denominations are reducing or eliminating vital programs. Competition for the charitable dollar is increasing exponentially. *The Millionaire in the Pew* opens an exciting door of opportunity to pastors and church leaders to mine a rich vein of wealth for the Church and its programs.

In the pages that follow, Russ Wilson builds on the premise that in spite of the current economic challenge there is wealth in the churches that, in his words, "is not being harvested." Wilson calls attention to the so-called "trillion-dollar transfer," the unprecedented transfer of huge amounts of wealth from the parents of the baby boomers to the 'boomers and from them to their offspring, presenting the churches with a rare opportunity to raise additional gifts. He asserts that, "clergy are in a unique position to do major gift fundraising," and makes the case that if clergy and denominational leaders were trained in, and motivated to do, fundraising — as practiced by professionals — they could raise millions of additional dollars for the Church, its ministries and missions.

This book provides a wake-up call for clergy. Wilson addresses the reasons why many clergy are reluctant to become involved with money and fundraising. A goal of the book is to educate clergy so they are comfortable and effective doing major gift fundraising. He provides step-by-step instructions for how to identify wealthy church members and how to work with them. This book will teach pastors and church leaders how to lead prospects to making six-and-seven-figure current and deferred gifts.

Wilson is fully qualified to address these critical issues and to relate to clergy. He spent many years in ministry in the Iowa Conference of the United Methodist Church as pastor and as a conference program staff member. He also spent many years doing professional fundraising at Morningside College in Sioux City, Iowa, and at the Iowa State

University Foundation in Ames, Iowa. At Iowa State he participated in a successful $450 million capital campaign. After retiring, Russ directed a campaign that raised $3.5 million to upgrade the campsites in the Iowa Conference of the United Methodist Church.

Wilson shares many of his personal experiences as a fundraiser and draws on the groundbreaking work on fundraising training for pastors and conference ministers now required by the United Church of Christ. Current research on giving done by the prestigious Center on Philanthropy at Indiana University provides important information regarding people's motivation for giving.

I believe this book will make a significant contribution to the Church by empowering pastors, denominational executives, and church leaders to provide critical financial resources to continue and expand its ministry and mission.

Bishop Julius Calvin Trimble
Resident Bishop
Iowa Area at the United Methodist Church

CONTENTS

1   **INTRODUCTION**

7   *Chapter One*
        An Attitudinal Metamorphosis — Fundraising As Ministry

15   *Chapter Two*
        The Apostle Paul — A Model Fundraiser

19   *Chapter Three*
        Clergy, Wealth and Transformation

33   *Chapter Four*
        Bishops and Denominational Executives — A Huge Opportunity

41   *Chapter Five*
        The Millionaire in the Pew

53   *Chapter Six*
        Deferred Gifts — The Motherlode

57   *Chapter Seven*
        The Real Reasons Why People Give

69   *Chapter Eight*
        Persuasion — The Art of Getting the Major Gift

77   *Chapter Nine*
        Preparing For and Making a Successful Call

85   *Chapter Ten*
        Building an Effective Major Gift Program

91   *Chapter Eleven*
        A Wide Lens Perspective

97   *Chapter Twelve*
        A Bald Eagle Feather and a Village in India — Generosity

107   **ACKNOWLEDGEMENTS**

108   **APPENDIX**

112   **BIBLIOGRAPHY**

114   **INDEX**

INTRODUCTION

In my years of ministry and professional fundraising I became convinced of two important factors. One, is that there is untapped wealth in the Church. The second factor is that pastors, priests, rabbis and denominational leaders are in a unique position to raise major funds for the Church.

For several years I have considered the possibility of organizing a seminar for clergy on fundraising and/or writing a book on the subject. I discussed the possibility with several of my clergy friends and they felt that such a work was timely and needed. The current economic crisis and the challenge it poses to many churches and church-related programs affirms the need for a book of this nature.

So, I began to do research and to review the material in a file that I had been gathering for several years. During this time I felt somewhat alone. I knew that many clergy would rather have a root canal than get involved with fundraising. Although many books and articles have been written about fundraising I was not aware of any work that provides fundraising education specifically for clergy.

And then, Dave Beery, one of the men in my monthly lunch bunch sent me an article from a United Church of Christ (UCC) newsletter. The article described that denomination's pioneering program to educate and motivate clergy and church leaders to do fundraising. The article quoted Rev. Stephen Gray, the Conference Minister of the Indiana-Kentucky Conference of the UCC.

In the article, the Rev. Gray identified himself as "one tough S.O.B. (son of a banker)." "Still," the article goes on to say, "When it came time for the minister to talk dollars and cents with his former congregation in Nashville, Tennessee, he blanched."[1] "I wanted nothing to do with money," said Gray. However, he has a totally different attitude today. As the head of a conference and with responsibility for the fiscal health and viability of a section of the denomination, he… "Is spearheading an effort to get UCC leaders — from the denomination's general minister and president to local church pastors — comfortable with one of the last modern taboos: soliciting donations."[2]

With the support of Rev. John Thomas, General Minister and President of the UCC, the denomination has contracted with the Lake Institute on Faith and Giving at the Center on Philanthropy at Indiana University. They have developed seminars on fundraising for conference ministers, conference staff, pastors, and lay leaders on one of the challenging issues facing the Church today — raising funds.

Rev. John Thomas put it succinctly when he said, "There's a new culture around how we fund mission and ministry in the Church. We can't simply hope that the way it used to be is going to come back."[3]

I had to meet Stephen Gray and learn more about their program. I called his office and made an appointment. We met in his office in Indianapolis. He was gracious and generous with his time and knowledge acquired in years of experience promoting giving in the Church. I will elaborate on the findings of a study done by the UCC and their creative plan of action later. Gray was very supportive of my effort to write the book and suggested several helpful sources of information.

Many mainline denominations are declining in membership. Baby boomers have different attitudes toward large organizations, including the Church, and are more selective with their charitable gifts. The costs of medical and hospital insurance for church staffs continue to increase exponentially. At the same time the costs of fuel for heating and air conditioning have reached all time highs. If that were not enough, the country is in the throes of a recession. No one can predict its negative impact on the Church.

In the past, religious causes and institutions received nearly fifty percent of all philanthropic contributions. That percentage fell to less than thirty-three percent in 2006.

Numerous news sources report that churches and synagogues across the country are struggling with finances due to the recession. Some high-visibility churches like the Crystal Cathedral in Los Angeles have declared bankruptcy. Denominations have reduced staffs and scaled down or omitted programs. Local churches have reduced budgets and staffs in order to remain solvent.

As if that weren't enough, competition for the charitable dollar is increasing exponentially. According to Lyle Schaller, "The new face of American philanthropy is distinguished by an unprecedented level of competition for the charitable dollar. This has created a high stakes game in which only a few thousand charitable, educational, and religious organizations can play at that high level of sophistication."[4] Every college, university, community college, seminary, art center, social agency, scholarship program, health agency, the Red Cross, and even an organization whose mission is to plant trees, is competing with the Church for the charitable dollar.

Patrick Rooney, Executive Director of The Center on Philanthropy at Indiana University, reminds us of the fierce competition for money facing the Church. This stark reality underscores the need for clergy and denominational executives to actively embrace fundraising.

"Each year, donors must choose among more charitable causes. There were 626,225 registered 501(c)(3) non-profit charitable organizations in the United States in 1995.

That had increased an extraordinary 67 percent by 2005, when there were 1,045,979 such organizations."

Rooney continues, "With this proliferation, there are more nonprofits out there asking, and people are continuing to give."[5]

One very effective way to attack these problems is to train clergy and church leaders to do fundraising. If they are educated to identify wealth, to cultivate wealthy parishioners, and to effectively present the needs of the Church, pastors can be very successful in soliciting gifts. This book was written with the goal of educating and motivating pastors and church leaders to do just that.

Please note that although this book was written and published during the recession of 2008–2011, the goal was not specifically to provide a solution to church finances during the recession. The purpose was and is to train clergy to do effective fundraising over the years as an integral and ongoing part of their ministry. That practice will not only help the Church meet its budgetary obligations, but also will make it possible to increase ministries and missions over time.

As I began to organize the material for the book, I realized that the information applies to several aspects of stewardship and fundraising, including emphasizing generosity, increasing skills of persuasion, and cultivating wealthy parishioners. For example, the chapter on persuasion will help pastors become more effective in motivating people to give at all levels, not only at major gift levels.

In one sense, this book is "Fundraising 101." Although its focus is to educate clergy, its contents apply to anyone who is responsible for raising funds or aspires to raise funds. In the following pages, the reader will receive the benefit of my twenty-three years of professional fundraising. I am volunteering to be your mentor, your coach, in fostering generosity and providing additional financial resources for your congregation or non-profit cause.

My seminary education did not include fundraising. I had "on-the-job training." Fortunately, I had some very good teachers and mentors who helped me along the way. During my years of fundraising at Morningside College and at Iowa State University, I had the benefit of attending several seminars and workshops on professional fundraising. At Iowa State University, I had the opportunity of working with and learning from some of the most successful fundraisers in the business. In this book I have tried to consolidate those learnings and experiences for your benefit and the benefit of your congregation or denomination.

After I retired from Iowa State University, I was asked to conduct a campaign to upgrade and expand the camp and retreat sites sponsored by the Iowa Conference. During that time I called on an estimated 150 ministers. Some of them were reluctant to get involved with the campaign. Some expressed concern about our practice of going to people personally, making the case for the camps, and presenting a written proposal and an "ask" of a specific amount. ("The ask" is a strange term, but it is the term used by professional fundraisers to describe a request of a specific amount.) A few clergy refused to participate in the campaign and many had no concept of professional fundraising practice.

During the camps campaign my staff and I discovered there are many wealthy couples and individuals in the Iowa Conference of the United Methodist Church. They represent only a small percentage of their congregations and they are not present in every parish. But, they are there. There is unidentified and untapped wealth in the churches that could, if harvested, meet many of the churches' needs. There is much evidence that there is substantial wealth in other denominations. The challenge for clergy and denominational leaders is to learn how to harvest those resources. I am convinced that in many cases the pastor is the key to generating those resources for the benefit of the Church. You, pastors, church leaders and denominational leaders, are the keys!

If you still have doubts about the potential for fundraising in the churches, listen to Patrick Rooney's words of encouragement:

> "The future of giving looks bright. As the baby boomers grow older, researchers expect a huge transfer of wealth from the 'boomers to their children and to nonprofits — a process known as the 'trillion-dollar transfer.' Charities will receive between $6.6 trillion and $27.4 trillion in charitable bequests, plus another $14.6 to $28 trillion in individual gifts, from 1998 to 2052, according to estimates by John J. Havens and Paul G. Schervish at the Center on Wealth and Philanthropy at Boston College. Whether or not these estimates ultimately prove precisely correct… they suggest a future trend of a large transfer of wealth…. The relatively rapid growth in foundation giving and bequest giving suggests that, the transfer has already started. Nonprofits need to prepare for the infusion of bequests and cash from this transfer of wealth."[6]

In Iowa and the Midwest, individuals and couples hold farm land valued in the millions, if not billions. The "trillion-dollar transfer," the largest transfer of wealth in this country's history, is in process. The older owners of land are passing their assets to their offspring, the baby boomers, and the boomers to their offspring. Very few of the offspring wish to become farmers, or are interested in farming. At the same time there are charitable gift plans and mechanisms that can benefit the donors by giving the land to the Church and other charitable organizations. Enlightened pastors and denominational executives can help to educate parishioners on those opportunities and persuade parishioners to donate land to the Church.

In conducting the campaign to raise funds for the camp and retreat sites in Iowa, we identified dozens of millionaires. It took some research, some detective work to find them, but we found them. It is reasonable to expect there are millionaires in most larger congregations in all denominations.

If you are a clergy person you have great potential for raising major gifts for your church and its programs. You have the trust and confidence of your people. If you are doing your job, you have a relationship, perhaps a very close relationship, with your congregants. If you don't know them already, you are in a position to get to know them and to learn a great deal about their values, interests, and financial assets. In your daily pastoral functions you have opportunities to cultivate wealthy parishioners. After completing this book you will know how to go about approaching your parishioners and leading them to make major contributions to your cause. You have huge power to generate funds that can change the Church and change the world! This book will help you unleash that power.

The following chapters are intended to help you reconsider your attitudes toward money, and wealth, and to form more positive attitudes toward active fundraising. The chapters are also intended to help you develop a robust sense of generosity in your congregation, to hone your skills of persuasion, and to be able to harvest abundant gifts for and through your church, synagogue, or denomination.

---

1   *United Church News*, February–March 2008, A16

2   Ibid.

3   Ibid.

4   Schaller, Lyle, *The New Context for Ministry*, Abingdon Press, Nashville, TN, 2002, 161

5   Rooney, Patrick, "Four Trends in Giving," *Philanthropy Matters*, June 2006, Volume 14 (2), Center on Philanthropy, Indiana University, Indianapolis, IN, 13

6   Ibid.

Chapter One

An Attitudinal Metamorphosis — Fundraising As Ministry

"Philanthropy is the mystical mingling of a joyful giver, an artful asker, and a grateful recipient."
REV. DR. DOUGLAS M. LAWSON

"Speaking the truth in love is part of the ministry of stewardship and fundraising, whether or not it amounts to an effective strategy." REV. DR. DAVID RUHE

In their research, Smith, Emerson and Snell interviewed twenty-six clergy from a variety of denominations. Some of those interviewed expressed negative attitudes toward money and stewardship. Some of the pastors interviewed expressed "varying degrees of frustration with the issue of financial giving."[1] The report continues, "Very often as our interviews unfolded, pastors also began to express feelings of helplessness, annoyance, and aversion to the issue [stewardship]."[2] "Others seemed uncomfortable because they viewed finances as 'unspiritual.'"[3]

There are no doubt many reasons why clergy are averse to stewardship and we will discuss some of those reasons in Chapter Three, *Clergy, Wealth and Transformation.* However, the position that stewardship and fundraising are 'unspiritual' deserves special attention.

Let's call upon several reliable and knowledgeable witnesses to testify to the fact that stewardship, raising funds for church and humanitarian causes, and fundraising can be very spiritual activities. They will argue that fundraising by a pastor, priest, rabbi, or denomination executive can be as spiritual as baptizing a baby or serving communion.

The defense calls a witness who represents the teachings of the Bible.

Defense: Will Witness Number One please take the stand.

Defense: Witness Number One, in your opinion, does the Bible support the assertion that fundraising for church and humanitarian causes qualifies as spiritual or spirit-filled activities?

Witness: The Old and New Testaments teach in many ways that the Earth and all of life are the Creations of God. All of our possessions, including our money, are God's possessions. According to the teachings of Jesus, Christians are responsible to use those resources to take care of one another and others in need. The parable of the Good Samaritan supports that teaching.

Defense: If money is used as a means of helping others, a spirit-filled activity, doesn't it follow that to raise funds for those purposes is a spirit-filled activity?

Witness: Yes, of course.

Defense: Thank you, you may step down.

Defense: Will the next witness, a representative of the Apostle Paul, please take the stand.

Witness: I refer to II Corinthians Chapters Eight and Nine. Those chapters record Paul's and Titus' fundraising among the churches of Macedonia, activities on behalf of the Corinthian Church. It is clear to me that Paul and Titus were actively engaged in raising money for the churches. I submit a copy of Chapter Two of this book as evidence.

Defense: Thank you, you may step down.

Defense: We now call to the stand Mr. Harry Stout, who is an authority on the life of George Whitfield, an influential leader of the early Methodist movement in the United States. In his biography of Whitfield, Stout relates Benjamin Franklin's experience of Whitfield's ministry.

Witness: Whitfield was a powerful preacher who drew huge crowds. According to Franklin, Whitfield decided to build an orphanage in Atlanta, Georgia. The charismatic evangelist preached about the need for an orphanage and raised thousands of dollars to support it. Whitfield was a shameless and very effective fundraiser. [Although Stout discusses Whitfield's fundraising from the pulpit, it is reasonable to assume that Whitfield also approached many wealthy believers personally and asked them to support the orphanage.][4]

Defense: Thank you, you may step down.

Defense: The next witness is a representative of Reverend Stephen Gray, a former pastor and former Conference Minister of the Indiana-Kentucky Conference of the United Church of Christ (UCC), now retired.

Witness: "The Reverend Stephen Gray always considered himself one tough S.O.B. (son of a banker).... Still, when it came time for the minister to talk dollars and cents with his former congregation in Nashville, Tennessee, he blanched. 'I wanted nothing to do with money,' said Gray."[5]

[However, Stephen Gray saw the writing on the wall — or, more likely, the red ink on the page. He is "spearheading an effort to get UCC leaders — from the denominations general minister and president to local church pastors — comfortable with one of the last modern taboos: soliciting donations. The UCC, in cooperation with the Lake Institute on Faith and Giving, at Indiana University, is offering workshops for clergy and church leaders to meet the challenge of providing adequate funds for the church's programs."][6]

Defense: Thank you, the witness may step down.

Defense: The next witness is prepared to present statements of several pastors who were interviewed in research done by workshops for clergy and church leaders.[7]

Witness: "Some of the pastors with whom we spoke held the view of money and giving as an essential part of faithful, daily Christian living that must be addressed confidently by the Church in a natural, holistic manner. 'It's a part of life,' they said. Pastors in this *Live-the-Vision* approach saw talking about financial giving as merely another one of the many aspects of Christian life that they are called to address."[8]

"One pastor put it this way: 'I think that giving money is a part of building the kingdom of God, and the role of us Christians is to help build his kingdom. And so, when you put that into perspective, what is our role? Then giving is just a piece of it. It's just a piece of the praise. It's a piece of the worship.'"

"Giving was described by *Live-the-Vision* pastors as a means of truly honoring God, of allowing God to be present in all aspects of one's life, including one's use of money. 'Giving money is allowing God to be God over all of your life,' said one, 'and not part of your life, but all of your life.' Another agreed: 'You look at your checkbook and see how you're using your money, and that's a reflection of your spiritual life.'"[9]

Defense: Witness, the pastors that you have quoted make the case that to give money to support churches and to feed hungry people and respond to other human needs is a spiritual process. Would you agree?

Witness: Yes, of course, I agree.

Defense: Thank you, you may step down.

Defense: Now, we call to the stand the next witness, a long-time friend of an eminent clergyman-fundraiser, the Rev. Dr. Clarence Tompkins. This friend, whom we will call Chess, reads from *Dream No Little Dreams,* an account of the 50-year history of Friendship Haven, a retirement residence in Fort Dodge, Iowa.

> *Witness:* "Tompkins not only gained a healthy work ethic, he learned much about the art of fundraising. His father spent part of his ministerial career raising funds for mission causes across the land, helping the Methodist Hospital in Sioux City, the Methodist Camp in Okoboji, the Wesley Foundation, and Goodwill Centers all over America.
>
> 'Our house was one of wealth, not in money or possessions, but rich in the values that came with a spiritual home. Table talk was adult talk, as I learned about people's problems and how to help those people. Fundraising also was table talk, which brought a continual parade of dignitaries and spiritual giants into our home for visits,' Clarence fondly recalled. 'They were building farms; they were building colleges; they were building hospitals; they were building church camps; they were taking the words of Wesley seriously, *The world is my parish.*'"[10]

Clarence Tompkins was appointed to be the first Executive Director of Friendship Haven. He started with a plot of ground in Fort Dodge, Iowa, and virtually nothing else except his faith, his determination, and his vision of a loving home for older people. In the following three or four decades, Clarence exerted every effort to raise funds to build what is now a thriving retirement home, health center, long-term care center, and center for Alzheimer's patients in Fort Dodge.

If one has questions about fundraising being a spiritual activity, one needs only to review the ministry, mission, and commitment of Clarence Tompkins.

Defense: Thank you, you may step down.

Defense: The last witness is Russ Wilson, who reports his interview with Rev. Dr. David Ruhe, Senior Pastor of Plymouth Congregational Church, in Des Moines, Iowa.

Witness: While having lunch with my friend, David, I mentioned the fact that I was doing research on the subject of ministers and fundraising. David encouraged me and related that he had recently made a presentation to a group of clergy on the topic of "Stewardship and Fundraising as Ministry." As we talked it became obvious that he had done a lot of thinking about the subject. He was so clear and articulate on the issue that I asked if I could interview him for this book. He generously agreed. Here is the interview:

Russ: David, please share with me your thoughts about clergy and fundraising.

David: Talk about stewardship carries with it a built-in conflict of interest. It's one thing to say to people, "For the good of your soul, you need to give some of your stuff to me." I understand that we're trying very hard not to be saying the latter. But just right now the temptations are pretty powerful and every seduction begins with a seduction of the self.

Like most of my colleagues, thirty plus years ago I started out in ministry talking very little about money. At age 28, I became the Senior Minister of First Central Congregational United Church of Christ in Omaha, and there I began to undergo an attitudinal metamorphosis. Early in my ministry my suspicion was that the more I talked about money, the less it would be forthcoming. But I found myself thinking and talking about money because I came to believe that our relationship to our stuff is one of the biggest spiritual issues in our lives.

R: Why do you consider our relationship with our stuff as a spiritual issue?

D: It essentially has to do with what or who will be God. It's no accident of language that when we want to know how much money somebody has we sometimes ask, "What is he or she worth?" In our society money is often granted the authority to confer worth, status, identity and power. We put a dollar value on everybody's time, which is arguably the gift of life itself. People who have a lot of money get treated as they are really important, and they are sorely tempted to believe it. People who have very little money are treated as though they are unimportant, and they are sorely tempted to believe it. These are two sides of the same coin, as it were. Money claims the right to influence nearly everything we do. Money claims the place of God!

R: What part does consumerism play in this?

D: The perpetual drumbeat of consumerism tells us that we have a lifestyle — that we style and shape our lives according to patterns of consumption through which we create ourselves in some image or other. We are told to think of ourselves as self-creating autonomous engines of consumption. That's idolatry.

And we are often possessed by our possessions, both individually and collectively. Getting and protecting stuff becomes a preoccupation. From gated communities to conflict among economic classes to foreign policy driven by the desire to control resources; stuff has the power to take over our lives. Individuals' lives are increasingly consumed by work because their lifestyle expectations are so inflated. Greed squeezes out values like loyalty and equity and justice when it comes to relations in the workplace.

R: What do you see as the minister's role in dealing with these issues?

D: These issues so dominate people's lives that ministry has to engage them. We have a very different story to tell about who and whose we are; about what makes for a fulfilling life; about who is really at the center of the universe. Our story says that there is a key relationship between cost and joy in discipleship; that clinging to our stuff as though it were a life preserver is a sure way to miss what life is really all about — that there is more than enough for all if we will learn to share; that part of nurturing within us the image of a generous God is learning to grow in generosity.

R: How does the Gospel relate to these issues?

D: I can't imagine how one could possibly address the relationship between our lives and the Gospel of Jesus Christ without talking about stuff, about stewardship. At Plymouth [Congregational Church] we talk a lot about Jesus' admonition to love God with all our heart, soul, strength and mind, and our neighbor as ourselves. We talk about financial support of God's work both within and outside the Church as being an essential part of the life of discipleship — as important as justice and prayer and study and personal acts of kindness. We point out that we witness to what we truly believe by how we give of what God has shared with us. The most transparent theological document a local church produces is its budget; for individuals it's the tax return. We say that sort of thing all the time.

R: How do you see this as ministry?

D: I think it comes down to trying to speak the truth in love. If we believe that the love of God is the greatest power in the universe, that Easter is our best window to ultimate reality, then we have to name some of the powers and principalities with which the Gospel is in conflict.

I think often of the story of the Rich Young Ruler. It's probably my favorite stewardship text because it is so grounded in love. As the story is told in Mark, I think Jesus initially doubts the young man's sincerity; he bristles at the designation "good teacher" as though the man is being disingenuous. But as they begin to discuss what it really means to "inherit eternal life," — as I take it, to feel the presence and power and love of God in our lives in a way over which death holds no power — eventually Jesus begins to sense that the man really does yearn for this; as I think at the deepest level we all do.

So once Jesus believes that the young man is sincere, the text says, "Jesus, looking at him, loved him and said, 'You lack one thing.'" Can you imagine? One thing! Only one thing; go, sell what you own, and give your money to the poor, and you will have treasure in heaven; then come, follow me.

It means everything to me in Mark, where words are as precious as diamonds. Mark, "Mr. Immediately," says that Jesus spoke this out of love. He didn't turn to the disciples and snicker behind his hand, "Watch me nail this guy!" This young man was possessed by his possessions, and Jesus was proposing an exorcism. It's poignant, powerful, and touching.

But, as Dr. Phil might say, "How did that work out for you?" How did this challenge work out for Jesus, as a fundraising strategy? Apparently it didn't work very well. We're told that, "When (the man) heard this, he was shocked and went away grieving, for he had many possessions." Was that the end of it? We don't know. I'll bet some stories have been written about what happened in this guy's life after he walked away from Jesus. If they haven't been written, they should be.

Speaking the truth in love is part of the ministry of stewardship and fundraising, whether or not it amounts to an effective strategy. And we need to keep that always in mind.

R: Do you see any positives in the situation, any reason for optimism?

D: Yes, I am heartened by all of the discussion about making a case for generosity and focusing on the needs of donors as a way of inviting them into the spiritual richness of giving — treasure in heaven, if you will. I think that the old model of giving from duty certainly has its limitations and with our fetish for confidentiality most people aren't aware that the duty to give a certain percentage in response to God's generosity to us hasn't had a lot of traction with our folks over the years. Many of our people sort of accessorize with religion, anyway, and don't always see the urgency of what we're trying to do. So being much more intentional and effective in getting a message across is a good thing, and a new way for us to issue the summons to generosity.

R: I understand that Plymouth Church conducted a $3 million capital campaign in 2006. What role did you play in that campaign?

D: I was deeply involved in all aspects of the campaign from the conception of the dreams to the final celebration. I feel that a pastor needs to participate fully in all aspects of planning and promoting a campaign, including fundraising. The success of the campaign is due, in part, to the minister's complete and passionate commitment to the proposed project. I think my unreserved commitment to our addition was absolutely necessary.

R: Did you actually make solicitation calls on people?

D: Yes, I made nearly all of the calls on our top prospective donors. Our staff gathered information on prospects and the campaign committee helped to identify and qualify prospects.

I think that people who are able to make large gifts are more likely to contribute if the senior pastor calls on them personally. Many of them occupy, or once occupied, top positions in their careers and are accustomed to working with the senior officer of the organization. In this case, I'm that person.

Also, in this case, I think I had a grasp of the spiritual programs and services that would be possible because of the buildings that were being constructed.

R: Did you see yourself as a salesman in that role?

D: Not really. A part of sales, as I understand it, is selling yourself. Sales people work hard at making a good impression, of building a relationship. When I sit down with a couple in their home, I see my role as telling them how the programs that will be possible as a result of this effort will contribute to the spiritual life of our children, youth, adults, and families. I tell them how these programs will promote the Kingdom of God. I may be overly presumptuous, but I think I can do this as well as anyone in the congregation.

R: David, thank you very much.

Defense: Thank you. You may step down.

Defense: I rest my case.

At this point, it may be helpful to review what is meant by "professional fundraising." The following graphic lists the various steps or functions that are involved in fundraising as discussed in this book. (See the chart on page 14.)

---

1   Smith, Christian, Emerson, Michael O., and Snell, Patricia, *Passing the Plate,* Oxford University Press, Oxford, NY, used by permission of Oxford University Press, Inc., 103

2   Ibid.

3   Ibid.

4   Noll, Mark A., *The Logic of Evangelicism and the Challenge of Philanthropy,* Center on Philanthropy, Indianapolis, IN, 2007, 1

5   *United Church News,* February–March, 2008, A16

6   Ibid.

7   Smith, Christian, Emerson, Michael O., and Snell, Patricia, *Passing the Plate,* Oxford University Press, Oxford, NY, 2008, used by permission of Oxford University Press, Inc., 132

8   Ibid.

9   Ibid.

10   *Dream No Little Dreams… ,* Friendship Haven, Inc, Fort Dodge, IA, 2000, 7–8

STEPS TO SUCCESSFUL MAJOR GIFT FUNDRAISING

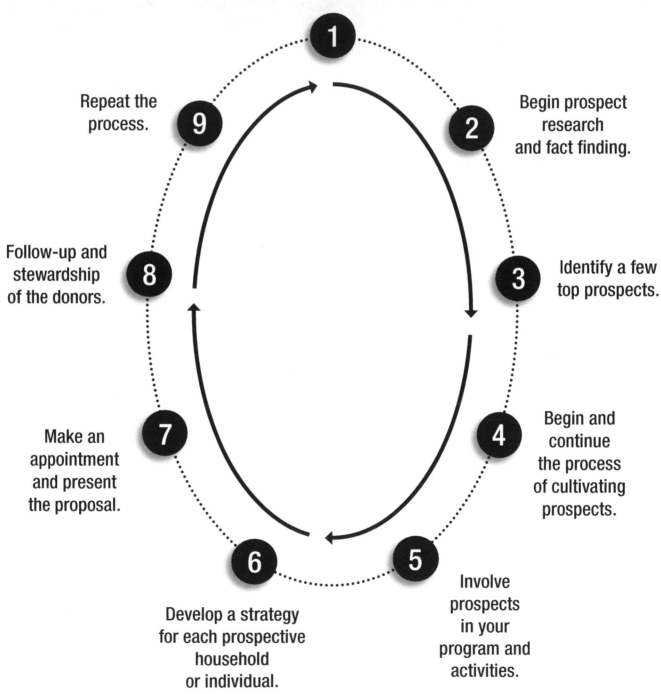

Create a long and short range plan
including goals, objectives and a timeline.

1

Begin prospect
research
and fact finding.

2

Repeat the
process.

9

Identify a few
top prospects.

3

Follow-up and
stewardship
of the donors.

8

Begin and
continue
the process
of cultivating
prospects.

4

Make an
appointment
and present
the proposal.

7

Involve
prospects
in your
program and
activities.

5

Develop a strategy
for each prospective
household
or individual.

6

Chapter Two

The Apostle Paul — A Model Fundraiser

"This generous work, which is being administered by us for the glory of the Lord Himself... "
II CORINTHIANS 8:19

"For the ministry of this service is not only fully supplying the needs of the saints, but is also overflowing through many thanksgivings to God." II CORINTHIANS 9:12

In order to establish a biblical base for the spiritual validity of fundraising we need look no further than to II Corinthians and the ministry of the Apostle Paul.

The National Development Institute, located in Columbia, South Carolina, conducted a conference on Faith and Fundraising in October of 2007. The focus was on fundraising in churches and church-related organizations. Jimmy LaRose, one of the founders of the Institute, key-noted the conference with a unique and interesting examination of the Apostle Paul's writings in II Corinthians, Chapters Eight and Nine (RSV).[2]

Before we consider Jimmy's interpretation of II Corinthians, Chapters Eight and Nine, I want to tell you about Jimmy. He is a consummate, highly-professional fundraiser. He and his partner in the Institute, Dr. Wesley A. Rediger, raise millions of dollars for organizations, including churches and church-related non-profits. These men are deeply committed to Jesus Christ. They are grounded in the Christian faith. They are students of the scriptures and passionate about teaching the processes and procedures of professional fundraising to pastors, priests, rabbis, and other religious leaders.

Here is Jimmy's presentation, entitled *The Essence of a Major Donor Ministry*:

Publicity Announcing the Philanthropy of Others
"Now brethren, we wish to make known to you the grace of God which has been given in the churches of Macedonia.... " II CORINTHIANS 8:1

The Impoverished Donor
"... That in a great ordeal of affliction their abundance of joy and their deep poverty overflowed in the wealth of their liberality." II CORINTHIANS 8:2

Giving Above and Beyond
"For I testify that according to their ability, and beyond their ability, they gave of their own accord." II CORINTHIANS 8:3

Desire to Participate
"Begging us with much urging for the favor of participation in the support of the saints." II CORINTHIANS 8:4

Philanthropic Priorities
"… and this, not as we had expected, but they first gave themselves to the Lord, and to us by the will of God." II CORINTHIANS 8:5

Donor Linkage (connection, relating)
"So we urged Titus that as he had previously made a beginning, so he would also complete in you this gracious work and will." II CORINTHIANS 8:6

Clients Served
"But just as you abound in everything, in faith and utterance and knowledge and in all earnestness and in the love we inspired in you, see that you abound in this gracious work also." II CORINTHIANS 8:7

Proof of Love
"I am not speaking this as a command, but as providing through the earnestness of others the sincerity of your love also." II CORINTHIANS 8:8

The Ultimate Gift
"For you know the grace of our Lord Jesus Christ that though He was rich, yet for your sake He became poor, so that you through His poverty might become rich." II CORINTHIANS 8:9

A Biblical Pledge Program
"I give my opinion in this matter, for this is to your advantage, who were the first to begin a year ago not only to do this, but also to desire to do it." II CORINTHIANS 8:10

A Clear and Concerted Challenge to Give
"But now finish doing it also, so that just as there was the readiness to desire it, so there may be also the completion of it by your ability." II CORINTHIANS 8:11

Desire and Ability
"For if the readiness is present, it is acceptable according to what a person has, not according to what he does not have." II CORINTHIANS 8:12

Financial Equity within the Body of Christ
"For this is not for the ease of others and for your affliction, but by way of equality at this present time, your abundance being a supply for their need, so that their abundance also may become a supply for your need, that there may be equality; as it is written, 'He who gathered much did not have too much, and he who gathered little had no lack.'" II CORINTHIANS 8:13-15

A Motivated Advocate
"But thanks be to God who puts the same earnestness on your behalf in the heart of Titus. For he not only accepted our appeal, but being himself very earnest, he has gone to you of his own accord." II CORINTHIANS 8:16-17

Celebrity Fundraiser

"We have sent along with him the brother whose fame in the things of the gospel has spread through all the churches." II CORINTHIANS 8:18

Consensus Among the Church Community

"… and not only this, but he has also been appointed by the churches to travel with us."
II CORINTHIANS 8:19

First Century Development Officers

"This gracious work, which is being administered by us for the glory of the Lord Himself… "
II CORINTHIANS 8:19

Financial Accountability

"And to show our readiness, taking precaution so that no one will discredit us in our administration of this generous gift, for we have regard for what is honorable, not only in the sight of the Lord, but also in the sight of men." II CORINTHIANS 8:19–20

Volunteer Advocacy

"We have sent with them our brother, whom we have often tested and found diligent in many things, but now even more diligent because of his great confidence in you."
II CORINTHIANS 8:22

Posturing the Team

"As for Titus, he is my partner and fellow worker among you; as for our brethren, they are messengers of the churches, a glory to Christ therefore openly before the churches, show them the proof of your love and of our reason for boasting about you." II CORINTHIANS 8:23–24

Demonstrating the Commitment of Others

"Namely, that Achaia has been prepared since last year, and your zeal has stirred up most of them."
II CORINTHIANS 9:2

Fear of Project Failure

"But I have sent the brethren, in order that our boasting about you may not be made empty in this case." II CORINTHIANS 9:3

Whatsoever a Man Soweth that Shall He Also Reap

"Now this I say, he who sows sparingly will also reap sparingly, and he who sows bountifully will also reap bountifully." II CORINTHIANS 9:6

Intellectual Giving vs. Emotional Giving

"Each one must do just as he has purposed in his heart, not grudgingly or under compulsion, for God loves a cheerful giver." II CORINTHIANS 9:7

Every Transaction is Powered by God

"Now He who supplies seed to the sower and bread for food will supply and multiply your seed for sowing and increase the harvest of your righteousness." II CORINTHIANS 9:10

Giving Produces Resources

"You will be enriched in everything for all liberality." II CORINTHIANS 9:11

Giving Produces Thanks

"Which through us is producing thanksgiving to God." II CORINTHIANS 9:11

Giving Produces Results

"For the ministry of this service is not only fully supplying the needs of the saints, but is also overflowing through many thanksgivings to God." II CORINTHIANS 9:12

Giving Produces Glory

"Because of the proof given by this ministry, they will glorify God." II CORINTHIANS 9:13

Giving Produces Testimonials to the Cross

"For your obedience to your confession of the gospel of Christ and for the liberality of your contribution to them and to all." II CORINTHIANS 9:13

Giving Produces Prayer

"While they also, by prayer on your behalf." II CORINTHIANS 9:14

Giving Produces Friendship

"Yearn for you because of the surpassing grace of God in you." II CORINTHIANS 9:14

Grace: The Ultimate Gift

"Thanks be to God for His indescribable gift!" II CORINTHIANS 9:15[2]

---

1   Note: All scripture references are from the *New Living Translation*, and used by permission of Tyndale House Publishers, Inc., Carol Stream, IL, 1996, 2004, and 2007

2   Ibid.

Chapter Three

Clergy, Wealth and Transformation

"… The Christian life is about a relationship with God that transforms us — it is about a deepening and centering in God… " DR. MARCUS BORG

"The lack of a financial gift needs to be seen as a symptom of a deeper spiritual problem within these people [current members of the church]." INA GRACE DIETTERICH

As we enter this chapter we are considering two avenues of transformation. The first is the transformation of the thinking and attitudes of pastors and religious leaders. Our concern is for those who are reluctant to or are downright opposed to becoming involved in stewardship and fundraising. If an individual is unwilling to participate in stewardship programming he or she is not likely to be open to the possibility of doing major gift fundraising. It is doubtful if he/she would be successful even if he or she did.

The second focus is the transformation of the thinking of our church members and households that moves them from minimal giving, or no giving, to making generous major and deferred gifts.

Let's first consider the transformation of pastors and religious leaders. We are not assuming that all pastors refuse to be active in stewardship and are candidates for transformation. Some of them, to their credit, and to the benefit of their congregations, are quite vigorously involved. Some of them may need to take the next step to doing major gift work, but they are already on the right track. If so, this book will lead them in that direction.

Now, in regard to transformation, Rev. Janet Long is a great example of a pastor whose attitudes and ministry have been transformed. Janet is an impressive woman. She is the pastor of Washington Avenue Christian Church (Disciples) in Elyria, Ohio. Parenthetically, if we were to choose a "poster child" for *The Millionaire in the Pew*, there would be no contest, Janet would be the one. I had the good fortune of attending the same break-out session with Janet at a national conference on stewardship in Indianapolis, Indiana, sponsored by the Ecumenical Stewardship Center. In that session, Janet told her story about ministering to wealthy people. In the first parish that Janet served, there was a young couple who were very active in the

Church. Janet got to know them well. One day the husband came to Janet's office and in general said, "My business is very successful. I make a lot of money. I want to begin to give money. Will you help me?" Of course Janet worked with him and he and his wife began to give generously to several church ministries and missions.

That interaction set Janet on a path of ministry to successful and/or wealthy people. She is both comfortable with and quite intentional about ministering to wealthy people. Later, when Janet and I discussed the subject of knowing what church people give, Janet said, "I don't know why pastors shouldn't know what people give. We know everything else about them — why not know about their giving?"

Although we did not discuss the subject of fundraising for major gifts, I am certain that if Janet's congregation needed funds or a special need came to her attention, she would not hesitate to share that need with her wealthy member friends. Thanks, Janet.

We are concerned with those who refuse to get involved, who see stewardship and fundraising only as necessary evils. If you qualify, we hope you will continue to read and to be open to the issues that are discussed in the following pages.

The pastor who refuses to involve himself/herself in the stewardship program of his/her parish is, unfortunately, avoiding an important aspect of ministry. He/She is missing the opportunity to develop a vigorous stewardship program and to engage in a rewarding ministry of major and deferred gift development. That is a ministry that could result in millions of dollars being contributed to vital causes and programs. He or she is refusing to use the power that could be used to effect some wonderful and desirable changes.

On the subject of why pastors are reluctant to become involved in fundraising, the authors of *Passing the Plate*,[1] Christian Smith, Michael Emerson, and Patricia Snell, report on interviews with a number of clergy from several denominations. In the book they discuss some of the negative attitudes or reasons why the interviewees are ambivalent about money or reluctant to involve themselves in stewardship.

One, is the "taboo" about discussing giving. Some listed the cultural taboo that in this culture giving is not to be discussed. Some interviewees observed that people simply do not talk about their giving habits. Some pastors find it difficult to break through the barrier that is related to the common myth that fundraising is a mysterious, unknown or forbidden activity. Nine times out of ten, in my career, when I met people and told them I was a professional fundraiser, they would say, "Oh, I could never do that. I could never ask people for money!"

I don't know how those attitudes developed and don't understand why they are so pervasive, but they are. The antidote is to recognize them as taboos, as unfounded thoughts like superstitions, or "old wives' tales," that seem to have a life of their own but simply have no foundation in reality.

In the Smith, Emerson, and Snell study mentioned before, of why people don't give more generously, some pastors told the interviewers they considered finances to be "unspiritual."

From our point of view, as related in Chapter One, that attitude is ill-founded and terribly unfortunate. We have made the case elsewhere in this book that stewardship and fundraising can be very spiritual, so we won't deal with the subject here.

In the Smith, Emerson, and Snell research interviews some pastors said that discussing money and promoting stewardship were difficult because they had no education on those subjects in seminary. For some pastors, this may be the biggest obstacle to involvement: the lack of education in stewardship and money.

Most of us would be terrified at the expectation that we go into the operating room and replace a broken hip joint or worn out knee joint. We have no education, no surgical experience. That's the way some pastors feel about raising money. The answer for pastors who are apprehensive about stewardship leadership is education and experience. There is nothing mysterious or magical about engaging in stewardship and discussing money. Education and experience will help pastors overcome that obstacle.

One respondent in the Smith, Emerson, and Snell interviews expressed the opinion that, I suspect, is shared by many clergy. That pastor said, "I'm not very good with money because I'm not very good with money myself."[2] It is fair to assume that if those individuals had some help with personal money management, they would be more comfortable with discussing stewardship and giving with their parishioners.

A few pastors alluded to the lack of support from their superiors. Apparently their denominations are not providing support, education, or clear policies about the stewardship expectations of pastors or church members. We cannot do anything about that phenomenon except hope that some of the bishops and conference ministers will read the chapter for bishops and denominational leaders in this book.

At this point I want to discuss what I believe are some additional obstacles to being involved in stewardship. I believe the fear of failure and the fear of rejection are causes — perhaps unconscious — for the reluctance of some individuals to put their hats in the ring of stewardship. You may recall your fear of diving off the high board for the first time. You can understand the influence of fear. The fear of failure, fear of appearing stupid, or fear of being rejected. Those fears are certainly understandable but they can be overcome with education and practice. Like learning to drive a car, or to roller skate, after you've done it a few times, the fear is gone and your self-confidence returns. Another remedy for fear of asking for money is doing a good job of researching your prospects, cultivating them well, and preparing a good proposal. By then your confidence will probably have overcome your fear.

A possible explanation for reluctance to involve one's self in stewardship and with wealthy constituents is that many clergy like me, grew up in low or lower-middle class families and had little or no experience with wealthy people. My dad suffered from health problems for most of his life and died at age 46 with a second heart attack. My mother worked full time most of her life. At times we barely made ends meet. I had no experience with wealth or wealthy people. I don't believe there was one wealthy individual or couple in the church we attended.

I recall a conversation with my friend, Rev. Dr. Larry Sonner, the former pastoral counselor for the Iowa Conference, now retired. We were discussing ministers' attitudes toward money. Larry grew up in modest circumstances. He grew up thinking that if people had wealth they were surely dishonest or crooked or both. How else could they get wealth? During seminary, Larry was assigned as a student pastor to a congregation that had many wealthy people in its membership. While working with them he discovered they were, in many ways, just like everyone else. They had their goals, problems, idiosyncrasies, hopes, frustrations and challenges just like the people with whom he grew up. I suspect that some of my clergy colleagues grew up like Larry and me with little or no experience with wealth or wealthy people. That may be one of the reasons that they are uncomfortable with wealth. The answer to that problem is to interact with your wealthy people and get to know them well and you will discover, as Larry Sonner did, they are much like other people.

Some clergy may feel uncomfortable because their efforts to increase giving may appear to be self-serving. They may wish to avoid being perceived as trying to "feather their own nest." The fact that some parishioners consider the minister to be an "employee" may tend to reinforce that attitude.

Actually, most people who have leadership positions in education, business, social work, or the professions, directly or indirectly, generate their own salaries. Sales people and accountants raise their own salaries. College presidents, YWCA and YMCA executives, doctors, heads of arts and social service agencies and non-profits, raise funds, including their own salaries.

Clergy are different in this regard; they receive no commissions, no bonuses for performance. Their income is not linked with their performance. Clergy raise funds to support ministries and missions that reach far beyond the purview of their local congregation. Fundraising for them is ministry, an act of spiritual commitment. They and their families are entitled, like everyone else, to be adequately supported.

And, even if a pastor were raising funds exclusively to pay her salary, she would be totally justified. Why? Because she is, by raising her salary, making it possible for her to provide pastoral leadership and service to her congregation. They are the ultimate recipients- the benefactors of her service. She is doing it for them!

Another factor that may prevent some clergy from getting involved in active fundraising is expressed in this excerpt from a church newsletter that was sent to me. The church or pastor was not identified. No doubt, he or she is a sincere and capable pastor. However, he/she doesn't understand fundraising. The article quotes:

> "Without voting to do so or realizing it, over the past several decades the leaders
> in many churches have substituted secular fundraising methods for Christian

stewardship procedures. Fundraising for non-profit groups in the community is as different from Christian stewardship as a bicycle is from an 18-wheeler. Both are valued forms of transportation, but they are not interchangeable. They accomplish two different goals." The article continues, "In the first place, stewardship as generally understood in religious circles includes the raising of funds and the management, use and distribution of funds for the support of the church and the assistance of others who need help."[3]

What is referred to as "secular fundraising," is neither secular nor religious. It is a system, a set of procedures, a methodology, whose goal is to promote generosity and to generate gifts. A goal of many professional fundraisers who conduct campaigns in churches today is to raise the needed funds *and to increase the level of giving beyond the duration of the current capital campaign.* When used by people who are committed to Christ and the Church, these "secular fundraising methods" are as Christian as what the pastor refers to as "Christian stewardship."

If the pastor intends to say that volunteer giving, practiced out of sincere commitment to Christ and the Church, represents "Christian stewardship," who could quarrel with that? At the point of identifying widely practiced fundraising procedures as "secular" or unworthy of Christian stewardship, he/she is simply wrong.

Professional fundraising procedures have been practiced in church capital campaigns and in church-related organizations for decades. And, by utilizing professional fundraising procedures, thousands of institutions have raised the funds they needed when general appeals have failed. When your family doctor determines his treatment is not solving your problem, he refers you to a specialist, who uses his specialized skills and experience to solve your problem. That's how I see the practice of fundraising as advocated in this book; the skills of a specialist, baptized by the Church, and practiced by pastors, priests, rabbis, and denominational leaders.

I have chosen not to elaborate on the Apostle Paul's and Timothy's direct fundraising practices to support my case. If you are interested, refer to Chapter Two, *The Apostle Paul — A Model Fundraiser.*

Another reason that some clergy may avoid fundraising is the demands on their time and energies. When one gets the calling done, visits the hospital or maybe two or three hospitals, prepares for the board meeting, leads the confirmation class, and works on the sermon, there may not be enough time or energy left to devote to fundraising. If, however, the pastor is going to be effective in raising serious money, he or she must make the issue a priority. Actually, major fundraising will not require a lot of time and energy, but the result will be well worth the effort.

Another compelling reason for joining the ranks of clergy fundraising is that the world has changed dramatically in the past decade or so, and it will continue to change. Many of the changes affect the churches and their ability to function. As Dr. John Thomas, the General Minister of the United Church of Christ (UCC), has said, "There's a new culture around how we fund mission and ministry in the church. We can't simply hope that the way it used to be is going to come back."[4] The UCC made the collective decision that their leaders and pastors should be trained in fundraising. The entire leadership of that major denomination made that decision and is engaged in providing fundraising education for their people. Here are a number of additional changes that must be taken into consideration:

1. The baby boomers, the largest segment of society today, attend church less often than their parents and, as a result, give less.

2. Baby boomers are more likely to distrust large organizations in business, government and the Church, causing them to be less likely to support the institution. They want to give to their favorite causes rather than to give to the "church."

3. Recent scandals of some religious and political leaders have caused some people to be less trusting of the Church.

4. Many donors today are more interested in the results of their giving than former donors. Thus, a more targeted and informed approach is called for.

5. There are more wealthy people in the U.S. today than in any other society. Some of them are members of a church, and are generous.

6. The population of older people in this country is increasing exponentially and many of them have wealth.

7. People are, in general, more sophisticated and informed about philanthropy and options for giving than in the past.

8. The fact that traditional modes of financing ministries, including tithing and systematic giving, have diminished in mainline churches.

9. The widening gap between the "haves" and the "have nots." The shrinking middle class and the concentration of wealth in more and more people, providing an opportunity to work with wealthy individuals.

10. A huge change and a phenomenal once-in-a-lifetime opportunity in the "trillion-dollar transfer" of wealth from the baby boomers to their offspring.

11. The ever-increasing competition for the charitable dollar. In 1995, there were 626,225 501(c)(3), charitable, non-profits in the U.S. By 2005, that number had increased 67% to an astonishing 1,045,979.

12. That one-to-one fundraising practice has "come of age" and is well accepted today.

13. And finally, people are well aware of the pressing needs for food, shelter, education, medical care and the prevention of disease. And, the fact that some people have indicated that they would give more if the Church would do more for others.

If you are still not convinced that you should take the big step and join with those who are actively involved in fundraising, consider these factors. The needs for support of local church programs and ministries are staggering. The needs for services to the community and the world are beyond imagination. At the time this is being written the news of the devastating earthquake in Haiti is breaking. That one catastrophe calls for millions of dollars in contributions.

Link the universe of needs with the "trillion-dollar transfer" that is in progress and the hard-to-be-believed potential for gifts to the Church that event presents. And, consider the fact that you may be the key — the only key — to harvesting some of that wealth to building the Kingdom, and you will surely step up and join the ranks.

While conducting a capital campaign in the Iowa Conference, the campaign staff interviewed many pastors to determine who in their congregations were prospects for major gifts. Many did not know who gave what, or who had potential for major or deferred gifts. They chose not to know that information. Some said, "If I know who is giving and who has wealth I might show them preference." The intent to treat all people equally, without prejudice, is admirable, but it blocks the pastor from conducting stewardship education and being involved in a ministry of fundraising.

A factor that challenges the "I don't want to know because I might show favoritism" attitude is the convergence of two powerful realities that are affecting the contributions to the churches! Those are the current recession and the exponential increase in competition for the charitable dollar. Pastors and church leaders can no longer maintain a "don't want to know" attitude toward people's giving and must become informed about their people's giving habits.

The Rev. Dr. Rich Pleva, the Conference Minister of the United Church of Christ in Iowa, read a draft of this chapter. On this subject he made this cogent comment, "Another indictment against the 'choosing not to know since I might show favoritism' is this. By this reasoning the pastor should choose not to know who in his/her parish is alcoholic, or divorced, who is terminally ill, or perhaps who attends church regularly. The pastor might run the risk of showing favoritism." Then, tongue in cheek, Rich says, "Perhaps the pastor should preach blindfolded and avoid that danger."

The "don't want to know who gives what" attitude assumes that clergy do not possess the self-awareness, professionalism, and the ability to monitor their behavior toward wealthy and very generous people. To openly, obviously, show favoritism or preference to any member for any reason would be unprofessional and foolish. However, it is possible to discreetly and unobtrusively relate to those people who have resources and to cultivate them without "showing favoritism." I believe the process of cultivating people and leading them to make significant gifts is a very spiritual ministry that can result in the spiritual transformation of wealthy parishioners and the generation of precious resources for the Kingdom.

Additionally, the rationale, "don't want to know," fails to recognize that an individual's or couple's giving is one of the few concrete, obvious, and reliable indicators of a member's or couple's attitudes toward the Church and perhaps of their spiritual health. The absence of financial contributions or a reduction in giving can be symptomatic of a deeper problem. It may be an indication that the Church is not meeting their needs or the family is experiencing financial or other stress. If a couple has a six-figure income or owns three apartment complexes and is giving $10 a week to their church that indicates the need for some spiritual guidance, education, cultivation or pastoral T.L.C., or, perhaps all of the above.

To refuse to be informed of her people's giving denies the pastor the opportunity to recognize her member's giving. A wise pastor, who is aware of her parishioner's giving, will find ways to express to those people appreciation for their generous contributions. As you read the subsequent chapters, *Persuasion — The Art of Getting the Major Gift* and *The Real Reasons Why People Give,* you will learn, if you don't already know, that most people want and need recognition. A pastor cannot recognize and express appreciation for what she does not know. Douglas Lawson emphasizes people's need for recognition in this poignant quote, "Like the impoverishment of sensuality, we lack healthy doses of genuine appreciation and heartfelt thanks for our good actions. Most of us need such thanks from others, and need to feel that we matter to someone."[5]

Imagine for a moment, that you are not feeling well. You go to the doctor. The nurse checks your blood pressure and pulse. When the nurse offers that information to the doctor, he/she says, "I don't want to know that information. If I know that, I might treat him differently." Or, imagine the director of an orchestra who declines to know who his most talented players are. Or, the head of a business who chooses not to know who his best salespeople are, or the administrator of a hospital who chooses not to know who his most skillful surgeons are.

"Wait a minute," you say. "My financial secretary or treasurer will not allow me to see the giving records. There is no way that I can know who gives and who does not." In that case, you need to have a serious discussion with that person or those persons. If that does not work, you need to take the issue to your official board or policy-making group. Use the arguments discussed in this chapter. Good luck.

Our former minister, Rev. Doug Peters, Senior Pastor of Walnut Hills United Methodist Church in Des Moines, used an illustration that provides a segue into the next issue. He recalled those metallic three-dimensional pictures of the '70s, that looked on the surface like spaghetti. But, as you fixed your gaze and relaxed your view, a beautiful eagle appeared with wings spread. Doug's point was that sometimes we need to look more carefully at a situation, story or event, to see its true meaning and beauty. In that light, if you are one of those who harbors negative attitudes toward wealth or who refuses to inform yourself about your people's giving patterns, I invite you to ask yourself these questions (better yet, write down the answers):

1. What were the financial circumstances of your family when you were growing up?

2. What were your parents' attitudes toward money?

3. What were your earliest attitudes toward money? What informed or caused those attitudes?

4. What are your attitudes toward money today?
   Positive 10 9 8 7 6 5 4 3 2 1 Negative. Why?

5. Do your personal finances or difficulty managing your own finances influence your attitude toward money?

6. How do you feel about wealth in general, and about wealthy people? How would you rate your comfort level on a scale of 1–10 with 10 being very comfortable?

7. Do you inform yourself about who is giving what to your parish, church?

8. Do you see people's giving as a kind of spiritual thermometer — an indicator of their spiritual growth and satisfaction with the Church or your ministry?

Obviously, your attitudes toward money, wealth and people of wealth will have a strong influence on your work with them. Your attitudes may make you highly effective with them, or totally ineffective.

At this point I hope you have a better understanding and assessment of your attitudes toward wealth and wealthy people. I hope that your attitudes are positive, because you are in a unique position to raise major gift funds for your congregation. Here's why: As a clergy person you are a natural for raising money, including major gifts, and you are uniquely positioned to do so. During your ministry you may have many opportunities to harvest major and deferred gifts by wills, trusts, and other mechanisms for transferring wealth.

In the profession, fundraising is often referred to as "friend-raising." People are more likely to give to "a friend" — someone whom they know and trust. In the chapter on persuasion, we deal with the process of cultivating and developing a relationship of trust and respect with prospective donors. Professional fundraisers often work for months or years to develop a quality relationship with a client, especially when six and seven figure gifts are involved. In my career, I called on some people for several years before I asked them for a major gift. That was especially true when I was seeking a large deferred gift.

One study I saw a few years ago indicated that it took an average of nine calls and contacts over an average of eighteen months to achieve a major gift. The study considered $25,000 and up as a major gift. Keep in mind that some fundraisers have to work with people all over the United States. Budget constraints limit the times they can go to Portland, Oregon, or Portland, Maine, to call on prospects. A pastor, priest or rabbi may have contacts with a prospect many times in a year, and be able to drive a mile or so to visit with a prospect. Pastor, priest, rabbi, you have a huge advantage!

In most cases your prospective donors know you well. You already have a positive, professional, perhaps warm and caring, relationship with them. They probably live within a few miles of the Church. They trust you. They know you have their interests at heart. They will believe you and seriously consider your request if you present them with a proposal. You already have two men on base and a hard hitter up to bat!

As a pastor, priest or denominational executive, you have excellent communication skills. If, as pastor, you are not the most skilled communicator in the congregation, you are one of the most articulate. You are an excellent candidate to present a case and make a solid argument for the project or program needing support. We're talking about home runs here, and you, the pastor are a heavy hitter.

Either by osmosis or by doing your research, as a pastor you know something about your people's resources. Chapter Five, *The Millionaire in the Pew*, will help you with your fact gathering research. That chapter will help you determine your prospect's interests and needs. It will also help you determine a reasonable level of gift request to present to them.

The entire process of obtaining major and deferred gifts is dependent upon you recognizing that to educate yourself to do major gift solicitation is a legitimate and, as David Ruhe and many others have argued, a spiritual function of ministry.

I believe that raising funds to support ministry and mission is as spiritual as praying, preaching, or serving communion. Money, as we have discussed, can be a wonderful resource for good. You may have some parishioners who have wealth or relative wealth. Those people may need guidance regarding the needs of the Church and some persuasion to move in that direction. Lovingly taking them by the hand and guiding them to the point that they make a generous gift or gifts, is a deeply spiritual, transformational process. It is not only a natural process for clergy to be involved in; it is an essential function of ministry in today's competitive environment.

I am not suggesting that you devote a lot of time to major gift work. And, you may not have any prospects in your current parish. On the other hand, you may have several prospects. In your usual practice of calling on people and maintaining contact with them you are already developing relationships and cultivating people. You are already taking positive steps toward becoming an effective fundraiser.

By discretely gathering and recording information about people's resources and interests (as outlined in Chapter Five) you will be able to accelerate the process and move toward approaching your parishioners for gifts.

I want to tread lightly here, but want to say this, however. Whenever you acquire a new set of skills, some new arrows in your leadership quiver, you become a more effective and more valuable leader. If you become known as an effective fundraiser and have developed those skills, that may open doors for you professionally. What could be better for you than to be assigned to or called to a parish where you can further develop and utilize your skills to the benefit of that congregation? I can assure you that if the leaders of a parish were considering the qualities of different candidates, and learned that one is highly skilled in promoting generosity and in obtaining major gifts, that person's name would go to the top of the list.

My hope is that this book will inspire you to get involved in the process of developing generosity and generating major gifts for your congregation. You can do it!

Dr. Marcus Borg lectured in Des Moines a few months ago. In a lecture he stated, "Consistent with a definition of religion as a means of ultimate transformation… the Christian life is about a relationship with God that transforms us — it is about a deepening and centering in God… ”[6] If our task as pastor, priest or rabbi includes the transformation of our wealthy constituents we must inform ourselves about their giving habits. We must concern ourselves with their spiritual growth, their transformation.

We have discussed the process of transformation of those who have resisted being involved in stewardship education and promotion. We have also agreed that in order to be effective in promoting generosity and giving, the clergyperson must concern him/her self with the giving habits of his/her congregants. Now, we turn to the transformation of our wealthy members and other potential donors.

The fact is that much of this book is devoted to that transformation. We have agreed that stewardship and fundraising are spiritual and essential aspects of ministry. The identification of wealthy members will be discussed later. The cultivation of prospective donors will also be discussed. What motivates people to give to the Church will be discussed at length in Chapter Seven. And, the general topic of generosity and the methods of promoting giving will be discussed. Those are ways of transforming our wealthy people so they understand the joys of giving, the deep satisfaction of helping others, and the emotional, physical and spiritual benefits of altruism. Keep reading.

We have also dealt with the transformation of the pastor's attitudes toward stewardship and fundraising. There is another subtle, but extremely important, aspect of clergy transformation that is called to our attention by Janet and Philip Jamieson in their excellent book, *Ministry and Money: A Practical Guide For Pastors.*[7] They make the case that many clergy tend to send the message that "money is bad and businesspeople are greedy." The Jamiesons state that when church members are "commissioned" to do work in the Church, the message heard by working and businesspeople is that work in the Church is "spiritual" and that their Monday-through-Friday work, outside of the Church, is *not* "spiritual" — and is suspect.

The Jamiesons discuss research with clergy done by Laura Nash and Scotty McLennan.[8] In interviews with many clergy they found that a significant number of clergy have negative attitudes toward business and businesspeople. As a result, businesspeople often feel ignored and neglected by clergy. They found that little is done by clergy to recognize the legitimacy of business and less is done to equip businesspeople to relate their faith to their daily work experiences. Nash and McLennan suspect that some of the negativity is generated by seminary professors who point out to their students the tragic practices of some multi-national corporations, with the result that graduates tend to categorize all business and businesspeople as "bad guys."

The tragic result is that many Christians in business and commerce experience a lack of support from their churches. Many of them feel that their churches are not providing them the theological and moral tools for integrating their faith in their workplaces. In an attempt to fill their spiritual void, some have organized Christian support groups in their places of work.

This is not to say that clergy should not condemn the immoral practices of multinational corporations but should be careful to differentiate between those corporations and their practices and the Christian individuals in their congregations. Don't throw out the baby with the bath water.

The challenge is to recognize this perhaps unintended or intended behavior and to be proactive in including businesspeople and providing them the theological tools and pastoral care that they need and deserve.

Dr. Peter Harkema, Director of Denominational Advancement for the Christian Reformed Church, shared with me his experience with twenty successful businesspeople, each of whom Peter said had a history of generous giving to the Church. They were invited to a meeting. Peter wrote,

> "The purpose of the meeting was to gather them for a dialogue with the Executive Director of the denomination. The conversation was wide ranging and including their feelings about the churches they attend, the ministries of the denomination, and their opportunities to engage in developing both the ministry in their local church and at the denominational level. A theme that echoed throughout our time is their desire to engage in developing both the ministry in their local church and at the denominational level. Historically, they said the church expected them to fund ministry but they wish to be a part of developing the ministry. 'Don't just ask us to fund what "you" want to do; ask us to help you develop the concept and use our experience to make ministry better.' They were frustrated that the church has the expectation that they will bankroll projects without their input. Some expressed the concern that the church was afraid of their entrepreneurial instincts and that ministry was always best if the ministry professionals put it together. Listen to us. Engage us. Get us involved. All of these were core themes that came out."[9]

These quotes and the research that informs them underscore the stated assertion that many clergy have neglected businesspeople, many of whom are capable of making six- and seven-figure contributions. Failure to minister and relate to businesspeople is a terrible failure of pastoral care. I believe it is also a failure of channeling significant amounts of funds in the Church.

---

1   Smith, Christian, Emerson, Michael O., and Snell, Patricia, *Passing the Plate,* Oxford University Press, Oxford, NY, 2008, used by permission of Oxford University Press, Inc., 105

2   IBID

3   Comments from an unidentified church newsletter

4   *United Church News,* February–March 2008, A16

5   Ornstein, Robert E. and Sobel, David, *Healthy Pleasures,* Addison-Wesley Publishing, 1989, quoted in Lawson, Douglas M., *Give to Live,* ALTI Publishing, LaJolla, CA, 1991, 27

6   Borg, Marcus, Lecture in Des Moines, Iowa, 2007

7   Jamieson, Janet T. and Jamieson, Philip D., *Ministry and Money: A Practical Guide For Pastors*, Westminister John Knox Press, Louisville, KY, 2009, used by permission of www.wikbooks.com

8   Nash, Laura L. and McLennan, Scotty, *Church on Sunday, Work on Monday: The Challenge of Fusing Christian Values with Business Life,* Jossey-Bass, San Francisco, CA, 2001, 14–15, quoted in Jamieson, Janet T. and Jamieson, Philip D., *Ministry and Money: A Practical Guide For Pastors*, Westminister John Knox Press, Louisville, KY, 2009, used by permission of www.wikbooks.com, 180–181

9   Quoted from personal correspondence from Dr. Peter Harkema, 201

Chapter Four

Bishops and Denominational Executives — Challenge and Opportunity

"There's a new culture around how we fund missions and ministry in the church.
We can't simply hope that the way it used to be is going to come back." REV. JOHN H. THOMAS

"Conference ministers and the boards need to address and overcome their present ambivalence
about their responsibility to provide leadership in fundraising."
FROM A REPORT OF A STUDY CONDUCTED BY THE UNITED CHURCH OF CHRIST

In Chapter Three we addressed the issue of some clergy's resistance to becoming actively involved in personal fundraising. As a bishop or denominational executive you may have some of those same barriers. Since most denominational leaders are chosen from the ranks of the pastorate, it is not surprising that you would be harboring some of those attitudes of resistance.

At the same time, you must be acutely aware of the financial challenges that many congregations and denominations are facing. In his book, *The New Context for Ministry*,[1] Lyle Schaller provides an excellent description of the social, economic, attitudinal and population changes that are affecting the Church today. He clearly discusses the competition for the charitable dollar posed by secular and church-related organizations such as colleges, retreat facilities, seminaries, retirement homes, and social agencies. Schaller reminds us that secular agencies, including colleges and universities, art centers, hospitals, and many other organizations are on the streets every day of the year competing for the charitable dollar.

Earlier, we made the case that clergy are in a prime position to do development. Most of them are people-people. They have a quality relationship with their wealthy constituents. They can discretely cultivate their wealthy members. They are able to articulate the needs of the parish. They are recognized as leaders. The same and more can be said about denominational leaders. They possess those positive qualities and they have a position of authority and power. Perhaps more importantly, they are in a position to influence hundreds of pastors and church leaders. Leaders of denominations can be torch-bearers, role models for their pastors. I believe the potential for denominational leaders to cause millions of dollars to be contributed to their churches and denominations is truly huge.

Bishop Gerald Ensley, a former Bishop of the Iowa Conference of the United Methodist Church, once told this story: A football fell into the chicken yard. The rooster gathered the hens around and said, "I don't want to put any pressure on you, but I want you to see what some other hens are doing."

Parenthetically, I also recall another bit of humor that Bishop Easley shared. He made this statement at an annual conference meeting attended by several hundred United Methodist ministers and an equal number of lay leaders. "Ministers are," he said, "like manure; get them all together and they make an awful stink. Spread them out over the land and they do an awful lot of good." It brought the house down. Only a bishop could pull that off.

Now, back to the football/egg story. I don't intend to put any pressure on anyone either, but am pleased to refer again to what the United Church of Christ (UCC) is doing. According to an article in United Church News, the Rev. Stephen Gray, the head of the UCC's Indiana-Kentucky Conference, "… is spearheading an effort to get UCC leaders from the denomination's general minister and president to local church pastors comfortable with one of the last modern taboos: soliciting donations."[2] With assistance from the Lake Institute on Faith and Giving at Indiana University, the UCC has developed three- and four-day seminars on fundraising for their conference ministers, their staffs, their pastors and lay leaders.

As previously mentioned, according to Rev. John H. Thomas, General Minister and President of the UCC, "There's a new culture around how we fund mission and ministry in the church. We can't simply hope that the way it used to be is going to come back."[3] According to the article in the United Church News, philanthropic contributions to churches in the U.S. fell from nearly half in prior years to under 33% in 2006. "Research indicates that these trends in giving are experienced by most denominations and faiths."[4]

The UCC has recognized the problems of funding ministry and mission and has taken bold steps to attack those problems. The denomination provides us an excellent plan that addresses the roles and responsibilities of denominational leadership in fundraising. The UCC conducted an extensive study a few years ago. Among their findings were these:

"Throughout the system there is little awareness of or interest in denominational ministries [These are programs funded by the denomination]."

"There is deep ambivalence in the system about asking and even learning how to ask for financial support."

"We need to rethink board structure and membership to reflect new fundraising realities."

"Conference systems are, at best, ambivalent to fundraising as a major component of a conference minister's job description."

"The system has very limited experience in soliciting major gifts."

The report continues: "If we are to initiate a change in the system… there needs to be a coordinated training set of expectations for conference ministers around fundraising." And, "Conference ministers and their boards need to address and overcome their present ambivalence about their responsibility to provide leadership in fundraising."[5]

In the background statement of the study report the committee states the need for training for pastors in the skills and procedures of fundraising.

The study also addresses the need for an updated, correct method of funding the wider mission of the Church. "While past UCC generations could rely on churches and conferences to provide a voluntary tithe to the [wider mission of the denomination] with limited prodding by the national setting, decreasing [wider mission] revenues over the last few years indicate that this passive method is no longer tenable… The 21st century church must transform to meet these demands or risk losing resources for the diverse work of local churches, associations, conferences, and denominational entities, including board-based mission work that cannot be accomplished on purely local and regional levels yet require local and regional financial support to survive."[6]

In order to effect the desired transformation and renewal the report says the followings steps are to be taken:

> "… Leaders at all settings of the church — local pastors, conference ministers, national clergy, boards of directory — incorporate fundraising into their set of expected activities. Job descriptions of both paid staff and lay boards reflect this expectation and search/nominating committees stress importance of these expectations. National and conference ministries maintain well-publicized and easily accessible systems for empowering church leaders to meet this expectation… including, training opportunities, written guidelines, dissemination of best practices."[7]

The UCC has made it clear that the leaders of the denomination, in their case, the president, and the conference ministers, are responsible to participate in fundraising and to provide leadership in fundraising for their pastors. In effect, they are saying that fundraising is an essential and legitimate role of denominational leaders.

The UCCs are out of the gate and down the track. This visionary plan was initiated in 2007 when every one of the 38 conference ministers attended a four-day workshop on fundraising conducted by the Lake Institute. According to Stephen Gray, chair of the committee, the workshop was well accepted. In September of 2008, a follow-up seminar was held in Indianapolis, led by staff of the Institute.

Some other denominations may also be doing creative work in effecting transformation in fundraising and financing ministry and mission, but time will not allow me to research that subject. In the meantime, our hat is off to the UCCs. We will watch their program with great interest.

The potential for denominational executives to raise six- and seven-figure gifts is huge. As we have observed, many church members possess substantial wealth. They believe in the Church and are aware of the positive programs the Church supports. Some of them have no children and will welcome sensitive and well-informed guidance from their bishop or denominational executive. Those people trust their bishop or leader to balance their personal interests with the interests of the Church. There are plenty of unscrupulous people out there who would fleece every dollar from elderly, wealthy people. But church members can trust their denominational leader to keep their, the member's, needs in view while considering the needs of the Church.

It is not unrealistic to expect that the denominational CEO of a main line denomination in a typical-sized state could, after a few years of lead time, raise one to five million dollars per year in major and deferred gifts. And that, without investing a lot of time and energy.

Denominational executives have some huge advantages and one or two disadvantages in doing development. A major advantage is that some wealthy parishioners occupy top positions in business, industry and the professions. They are accustomed to relating to people at the top. Many of them would prefer to do business with the top executive. Some have super-sized egos and will be flattered by the attention of their bishop, or conference minister.

During the camps campaign when I called prospects to make an appointment for Bishop Palmer and me, very few declined. Most were pleased to have the bishop visit in their home or office. Another advantage is that people trust their denominational executive to deal honestly and honorably with them.

Two negatives that executives have to face are: the challenge of determining who has wealth and the task of establishing a relationship with and cultivating those prospects. But, those problems can be solved.

As an executive of a denomination, you have pastors who know their members well and are in a position to do research and to identify wealthy prospects. If you request the pastors to identify those who have resources, you are accomplishing several objectives. You become a role model in fundraising to your pastors. You are encouraging the pastors to become involved in the process by doing the prospect research. At the same time the pastors are getting the information about prospects that they need in order to do development. Ultimately, you will obtain a list of your top prospects.

It may be presumptions of me to assume that I know anything that bishops or denominational executives do not know. But, I am going to run that risk. I have worked closely with several bishops and several college and university presidents. I have observed those top executives' commitment to and involvement with major gift fundraising.

I worked with Dr. Martin Jischke, former president of Iowa State University, currently the president of Purdue University, and saw him work his magic and raise seven-figure gifts from alumni of the University. If college and university presidents, Red Cross executives, heads of art galleries and social service agencies can raise millions for their agencies, I see no reason why denominational leaders cannot do the same.

If a bishop or denominational executive understands the tremendous power he/she has because of their position and is willing to get involved in raising major funds for their vision of the Kingdom, the following guidelines or suggestions may be helpful.

Step 1: If you have no experience or education in major gift fundraising, enroll in a seminar or workshop conducted by a reputable fundraising organization. The Lake Institute on Faith and Giving at the Center on Philanthropy at Indiana University has a great reputation and conducts seminars on faith and fundraising. In Columbia, South Carolina, the National Development Institute sponsors top-rate seminars. (Please refer to Chapter Eleven, *A Wide-Lens Perspective,* for more resources). If you cannot locate an event in your area, contact the development office of a hospital, college or university in your area. They will know about educational opportunities.

Step 2: Develop a list of twenty-five of your parishioners who have wealth. Chapter Five, *The Millionaire in The Pew,* will help you identify them, but you have the option of asking your pastors or priests, district superintendents and their administrative staff members to do the research and to identify those people for you. Get as much information about them as possible. The "Prospect Information Form" on page 50 will help you. In the process of persuading the pastors and others to identify prospects for you, you have the opportunity to inform them that your objective is to become involved in working with some wealthy people. You need to assure them that you will not try to divert funds from their church, but will attempt to increase contributions to the churches and the wider needs of the denomination. In the long run your efforts will help all of the churches accomplish their financial goals.

Step 3: Provide opportunities to meet those twenty-five wealthy individuals and couples and take advantage of every opportunity, even if it is small, to make contact with them. Make a point to call on, have coffee or lunch with, or visit with them in their home or office as often as reasonably possible. Even a phone call when you are in their area will help to maintain a relationship and to keep in contact with those people.

Step 4: Plan a luncheon, or a reception at your office facility or at a local restaurant and invite several of your prospects — not to ask for money or even to hint that is why you invited them. Share with them your dreams and goals for the denomination and the churches. Ask for their advice and their opinions. Express appreciation for their faithfulness and their participation in the Church. As you get to know these people you can begin to share specific needs with them.

Establishing solid relationships takes time. Don't push the river. An option is to invite the people to meet with you for lunch, dinner, coffee or dessert when you plan to be in their area. If you are preaching in a given area, or meeting with a committee or board, plan a get-together with your wealthy constituents the day before or after. You know, two birds....

Step 5: Phone calls, birthday cards, "thinking of you" cards, "congratulations on your new position or special honor" or "to keep you informed" notes all serve to establish and maintain a relationship. Fundraisers refer to this as the process of "cultivation." At a conference I recently attended, sponsored by the National Development Institute (mentioned in Step 1), speaker after speaker chanted the mantra: "Relationship, relationship, relationship."

If you have a relationship of trust, respect, and integrity with your people they will contribute to your cause if they are able.

Step 6: As a leader of your denomination and a leader of, and role model for, the pastors, you have an awesome opportunity to endorse and put your "seal of approval" upon the process of getting involved in major gift fundraising. By endorsing fundraising as ministry, as a spiritual effort, you will be inspiring clergy to become involved. The positive ramifications and potential of your endorsement and of their active participation are breathtaking!

If you think you cannot carve out enough time, energy, or attention to do these things, consider this. Martin Jischke was the president of Iowa State University for several years. His executive plate was always full — administrating a very large and very active university. However, he devoted 2–3 working days per month to development. He made calls with foundation staff members to cultivate donors and to ask for gifts. He considered fundraising to be a professional, legitimate and necessary aspect of his role as president. As a result, the University enjoyed unprecedented levels of gifts during his administration. Under his leadership, we successfully completed the largest capital campaign in the University's history — $450 million. Obviously, you are limited in the amount of time, energy and attention that you can devote to this process, but whatever efforts you devote to fundraising will pay rich dividends for the Kingdom.

A model of focused cultivation of prospects that I used at Iowa State University could be used by denominational executives. I was assigned to the College of Agriculture and was raising funds for that college. We organized a "Blue Ribbon Weekend." All "aggies" know that a blue ribbon at the fair is the best. We selected and invited to participate 30–40 individuals and couples whom we considered to have varying degrees of wealth — some were prospects for current major gifts, some for deferred gifts. We anticipated that thirty to forty individuals would attend, comprising twenty-five to thirty households.

The event was scheduled when Veishea, a big weekend celebration, and a concert or play were scheduled. We reserved rooms for them in a good hotel. We picked up the tab. During the day, presentations were made by the Dean of the College of Agriculture and a faculty member or department head. A planned gift person from the Foundation addressed the group. President and Patty Jischke were invited to dinner and Martin addressed the group. A few outstanding students were invited to lunch or dinner and placed at the tables so the guests could get acquainted with them.

Yes, it cost some money. But, it was well worth the investment. It helped to establish a positive relationship between the prospects and the Dean and myself. It also showcased exciting things the college was doing. It provided some soft, valuable information about gift giving and estate planning that was helpful to the participants. Soon after the event I followed up with notes to all of the participants and scheduled a personal visit within the next two or three months.

You may not want to plan such an extensive or expensive event, but a one-day program is possible. Begin at 10:00 am, have a lovely lunch and adjourn at 4:00 or 4:30 pm. You can accomplish many of the same objectives.

You have great potential for raising major and deferred gifts directly from prospects in your judicatory. However, don't overlook the unreal potential you have of promoting development among your staff and pastors, priests or rabbis.

You may choose to utilize the process followed by the United Church of Christ (UCC). That is, conduct a study of the state of resource development in your judicatory. Develop a set of goals and objectives in regard to resource development. The process will eventually lead you to the need to provide fundraising education for your staff and local leadership. I'm sure the UCC would share with you their plan for providing education for their pastors. (Please refer to the discussion on the UCC plan in the *Introduction*.)

Another strategy to consider is based on Rensis Likert's theory of organizational change. That is, the head of the organization selects a few, say seven to nine, of his most capable and creative people. He or she provides them with training in the subject area. She then surrounds them with support and resources. Careful records are kept of their progress and production. As they succeed and their success is made known in the organization others see the results. They want to receive the same training and support and to share in the success.

I could see a denominational executive selecting several of the most capable and creative pastors from each district, synod or diocese and sending them to a workshop on fundraising. An option would be to organize a workshop exclusively for them. The executive would arrange for records to be kept on those people's experiences — for future education and publicity. The bishop or denominational leader would meet with them routinely to discuss progress and to provide support. The program would be publicized in the denomination's newsletters and in other modes of communication.

As those people progress and develop their skills and expertise they could become trainers and mentors to others. Like the ripples on the pond, their influence would eventually spread out to other pastors and church leaders. However, this approach would be much slower than the UCC approach.

A word of advice is in order. Take aggressive action. This issue is extremely important. Time is of the essence. The "trillion-dollar transfer" is happening but it will not last forever. The door of opportunity is open. It's time to act. However, it will take time to change attitudes. It will take time to provide educational opportunities. Identifying wealthy prospects will take time, as will the process of getting acquainted with and cultivating them. It may be two or three years before you achieve any major gifts. It may be five or more years before you see any deferred gift results. Be patient. The process requires time, but when one of your prospects contributes a $1 million gift or leaves their estate to your denomination you will know the effort has been worthwhile. You can do it!

1   Schaller, Lyle E., *The New Context for Ministry,* Abingdon Press, Nashville, TN, 2002

2   *United Church News,* February–March 2008, A16

3   Ibid.

4   A quote from Dr. Tim Seiler, Director of the Fundraising School, Center on Philanthropy, Indiana University, Indianapolis, IN, quoted in *United Church News,* February–March 2008, A16

5   *Preliminary Findings and Recommendations,* United Church of Christ Council of Conference Ministries, Development Committee, United Church of Christ, 2

6   Ibid.

7   *Financial Transformation and Renewal Program, Request to the Lilly Foundation,* United Church of Christ, 5

Chapter Five

The Millionaire in the Pew

"I am opposed to millionaires but it would be dangerous to offer me that position... "
MARK TWAIN

"These people cannot be millionaires. They don't look like millionaires, they don't dress like millionaires, they don't act like millionaires — they don't have millionaire names. Where are the millionaires who look like millionaires?" FROM *THE MILLIONAIRE NEXT DOOR*

Identifying wealth can be challenging. While I was at Morningside College in Sioux City, Iowa, I called on a couple in Northern Iowa who had been referred to me by a clergy member of the Board of Directors. The couple had a casual relationship with a Lutheran Church in their town. Prior to my visit, they recognized the name of the college but that was all they knew about it.

I called on them and introduced myself. They were farmers. Their house was small and modest, bordering on sparse. The nap on the carpet was worn through to the threads in front of the couch and an over-stuffed chair in the living room. If I had determined their wealth by those observations I would have marked them off my list.

I called on them several times and got to know the husband fairly well. Once, I found him in the "shed." It was a huge metal building that housed several of the biggest and most modern farm machines available. It could have doubled as a John Deere showroom. In doing research I learned that they owned ten to twelve farms. In addition to being a very successful farmer he was an astute investor. They had no children with whom to share or to inherit their wealth.

He and I discussed sports and I told him what a great college Morningside is. Each year, in early December, I delivered a nice poinsettia plant to their home or had one delivered. I never asked for a gift. I didn't think the time was right. My objective was to establish a quality relationship with them. When he died he left a major bequest to several agencies, including Morningside. When I left Morningside, I lost contact with the situation.

The 2009 Spring/Summer edition of the *Morningsider,* the semi-annual magazine of Morningside College, reported that the couple, Leon and Helen Koebrick, both deceased, of Charles City, Iowa, left $1.3 million to an unrestricted endowment and $1.9 million to an endowed scholarship for nursing to the college. The bequest, totaling $3.2 million represented the largest estate gift in the college's history! A few cordial calls, a relationship, and a few poinsettias....

For the moment, let's assume that you are one of those clergy who have been reluctant to identify people in your congregation who have wealth. Perhaps, you simply have felt uncomfortable doing so because you had no training. In either case, this chapter will provide you the information, tools and, hopefully, the motivation you need to identify your wealthy constituents.

Before we discuss how to identify the millionaires in your congregation, we need to recognize the difference between being wealthy and being generous. Some wealthy people, some millionaires, are very generous. Some are not. Some are like Scrooge. Some who grew up in the Great Depression of the 1930s hold on to their assets like a drowning man clinging to a life preserver. Some people who appear to be wealthy are in debt up to their turtlenecks, others simply live beyond their means regardless of how much income they receive. Those people are not likely to be prospects. However, don't write them off; consider them a challenge. Love them, educate them, and cultivate them. They can be changed. Developing a major gift program is a long process. You can do it.

Some people who have very little wealth, if any, and have only moderate incomes, are very generous. They may be prospects for gifts of $5,000–$10,000 or more, spread out over 3–5 years. Their past record of generosity is a more reliable indicator of their potential than their limited wealth. Your current donors, regardless whether or not they have wealth, who have supported your church for several years, are among your best prospects. The Church is helping them achieve some of their personal goals. They are getting from the Church what they want or need. As a result, they are willing to give. In a typical congregation you are more likely to have five households with the potential for major gifts of $5,000–$10,000, than one household with potential for a gift of $25,000–$50,000. If you are fortunate, you have both!

What is considered a major gift in a large urban church may be far less in an inner city congregation. There are congregations in small towns and inner city neighborhoods that simply do not have wealthy members. For them, $1,000 might be considered a "major gift." In larger, urban congregations $10,000–$25,000 might be considered a major gift. You will have to determine what constitutes a major gift for your congregation and take that into consideration. Maybe you don't have any major gift prospects. Maybe you have several. Maybe the best potential in your current parish is for deferred gifts.

Obviously, the economic recession of 2008–11 has changed many things. It has caused many wealthy people to lose a lot of money. It has caused some people to lose their jobs and have to rely on their savings. These tragic results will change the environment for major and deferred gift work for some time. But major gift work involves a long process. The economy will recover. Some people will still be wealthy and others will achieve wealth. In the meantime, you need to create your system for doing research and retaining information on possible prospects.

One thing that has inspired me to write this book, and continues to excite me about clergy fundraising, is the tremendous potential for raising millions of dollars. These quotations from a recent book, *Passing the Plate*, will help us to comprehend that potential. (Although the quote relates to general or on-going giving, the figures also indicate the tremendous wealth in the Church and thus, the unbelievable potential for major and deferred gifts.)

"The up-side potential for good in U.S. Christian giving is immense, almost unimaginable. If American Christians were to give from their income generously — not lavishly, mind you, only generously — they could transform the world, starting right away. Ordinary American Christians have within their power the capacity to foster massive and unprecedented spiritual, social, cultural, and economic change that closely reflects their values and interests. In order to achieve such dramatic, world-transforming change, ordinary American Christians simply need to do one thing: start giving reasonably generously from their incomes, let us say 10 percent of post-tax income.… "[1]

"Fully grasping the capacity of ordinary American Christians to transform the world through generous financial giving requires comprehending the vast financial resources that are in fact at their disposal. But any comparative study of the number of Christian believers in different countries of the world and the financial incomes at their disposal reveals that *ordinary American Christians as a group are sitting on utterly enormous monetary resources*, both relatively and absolutely. In 2005, the United States contained approximately 226,624,000 professing Christians. About 140,070,000 Americans are Christians who report that their faith is very or even extremely important to their lives.… "[2]

"In short, well more than one hundred million Americans are professing and practicing Christians. The 2005 average U.S. household income was $47,290 for Protestants and $52,918 for Catholics. For regularly churchgoing Protestants and Catholics, average annual household income was even more, $50,138 and $57,791, respectively. Calculated out, self-identified Christians in the United States earned a total collective income in 2005 in the *trillions* of dollars. Christians in the United States who are actually members of churches earned a total collective 2005 income of more than $2 trillion. Christians in the United States who actually attend church twice a month or more often or who consider themselves strong or very strong Christians earned a total collective 2005 income of also more than $2 trillion. Needless to say, more than $2 trillion earned every year is a huge amount of money."[3]

In Chapter Six of this book, the unimaginable potential for deferred gifts to the Church is discussed. (Additionally, the potential for *major gifts* is also beyond comprehension.)

Some of the people in the $50,000 and up income categories have very little accumulated wealth. They spend what they make. Unfortunately, many spend more than they make. However, some of those people manage their money well and live within a budget. They also make wise purchases, and not only live within their income, but also allocate funds for the Church and charity. Some even manage to save some money. Obviously, they are an endangered species.

Lyle Schaller states that, "The number of American millionaires doubled during the 1990s. The number of Christians contributing at least $200,000 annually to charitable causes quadrupled since 1980."[4]

The book, *The Millionaire Next Door*, provides some good clues as to how to identify wealth. It defines wealth as the current value of ones assets, less liabilities. It defines people of wealth "as having a net worth of $1 million or more."[5] That description does not include annual income; it considers only net worth, which could include a residence(s), automobiles, rental property, a business, farmland, stocks, bonds, trusts, foundations, and other assets. "Based on this definition, only 3.5 million (3.5 percent) of the 100 million households in America are considered wealthy. About 95% of the millionaires in America have a net worth of between $1 million and $10 million."[6] The following are characteristics of millionaires quoted from *The Millionaire Next Door*:

- I am a fifty-seven year-old male, married, with three children.

- About one in five of us is retired. About two-thirds of us who are working are self-employed.

- Many of the types of businesses we are in could be classified as dull-normal. We are welding contractors, auctioneers, rice farmers, owners of mobile home parks, pest controllers, coin and stamp dealers, and paving contractors.

- About half of our wives do not work outside the home. The number-one occupation for those wives who do work is teacher.

- On average, our total annual realized income is less than 7 percent of our wealth. In other words, we live on less than 7 percent of our wealth.

- About half of us have occupied the same house for more than twenty years.

- We live well within our means. We wear inexpensive suits and drive American-made cars. Only a minority of us drive the current model year automobile.

- Most of our wives are planners and meticulous budgeters.

- As a group we are fairly well educated. Only about one in five are not college graduates. Many of us hold advanced degrees. Eighteen percent have master's degrees, 8 percent have law degrees, 6 percent medical degrees, and 6 percent PhDs.

- About two-thirds of us work between forty-five and fifty-five hours per week.

- We are fastidious investors. On average, we invest nearly 20 percent of our household realized income each year. Most of us invest at least 15 percent. 79 percent of us have at least one account with a brokerage company but we make our own investment decisions.

- We hold nearly 20 percent of our household's wealth in transaction securities such as publicly traded stocks and mutual funds. But we rarely sell our equity investments. We hold even more in our pension plans. On average, 21 percent of our household's wealth is in our private businesses.[7]

Obviously, these characteristics were listed more than fifteen years ago. Many things, especially figures regarding incomes, savings, and investments have changed. However, the characteristics of millionaires have probably not changed that much.

Farm families are in a special category. A farm couple may own or be buying farm land worth hundreds of thousands of dollars but have little, if any, discretionary funds. Farmers, like other vocational classes, vary from those who "barely squeak by," to those who achieve high profit margins. Nevertheless, after farm expenses, taxes, and living costs their discretionary funds may be very limited. An additional issue is that farmers don't know from year to year what their income will be.

In spite of those factors, many farm families are generous with their time and energy and do their part to financially support their church. Their potential for current major gifts may be nil. However, some of them, especially the older ones, have potential for major and deferred gifts, especially gifts of farmland. Those who own farmland and have no children are prime prospects.

What has been said about farm families remains true, but the farm economy has changed dramatically due to the emergence of ethanol as a gasoline additive. Farmers are currently receiving high prices for their products. That, no doubt, will affect the giving of some of them to their church. How long that will last is to be seen.

In regard to the potential for deferred gifts and the increases in bequests to churches, Lyle Schaller quotes the following:

> "What is the greatest single change in church finances from the emergence of the new American economy? If measured simply in dollar terms, that is the easiest question raised in this book. It is a ten digit number — $1,000,000,000. In 1992 Protestant congregations received at least one billion dollars more in bequests than were received back in 1952 after allowing for inflation. In other words, after allowing for inflation, bequests to congregations have increased by a billion dollars in forty years. This does not include the value of bequests received by para-church organizations, denominational agencies, church-related colleges, theological seminaries, or other christian organizations. For the calendar year 2001 Protestant congregations in the United States received well over $3 billion in bequests. That does not include cash contributions made by living donors."[8]

Schaller states:

> "For many congregations in which a substantial proportion of the adult members were born before 1930, bequests have turned out to be a welcome new income stream. Those who are comfortable balancing the operational budget of the congregation with gifts from the dead see these as the best of times. Those who are uncomfortable with the dead subsidizing the living call these the worst of times.... "[9]

Schaller continues:

> "Today's generation of mature adults (1) were heavily influenced by the Great Depression that inculcated the virtue of 'saving for a rainy day,' (2) grew up in a society that lifted up deferred gratification as a virtue, (3) worked in a rapidly expanding economy during the post-World War II decades when personal income rose at an unprecedented pace, (4) devoted more effort to learning and practicing the skill of saving than was devoted to learning the skill of spending, and (5) benefited from national economic policies that rewarded borrowers at the expense of savers in the 1940–85 era and that rewarded

savers during the 1985–99 era."[10]

Obviously, not all of the people born in that generation fit into those categories but many of them do.

However, there is a significant population of over-sixty-five people in the country today who are well off. That segment of the population "more than doubled from 16.5 million in 1960 to over 37 million by the end of 2001," according to Schaller.[11]

Years ago the College of Agriculture and, what was then called the College of Home Economics, at Iowa State University, had high enrollments. The agriculture or "Ag" students were primarily men; those of "Home Ec." were primarily women. The men tended to date and marry the women and vice versa.

Years later my good friend, Bob Basham, was raising funds from the women graduates of the College of Family and Consumer Science, the new name of the College of Home Economics. I was raising funds for the College of Agriculture. Occasionally, we targeted the same couple. The wife was a graduate of his college and the husband, of mine. Although we were competing with one another, Bob would occasionally, with a fiendish smile, remind me that it didn't matter how much money I raised from those couples. In most cases the husband would die first and the wife would end up with the wealth and would likely give it to his college.

That is true with much wealth in the Church. The men die first leaving the assets to their wives. Widows constitute a rich vain of wealth in the Church. Those who have wealth are prime prospects for major and deferred gifts.

While we are discussing wealth in the Church and the potential for solving serious problems with major gifts, I want to quote some important and eye-popping information. The source again, is the book, *Passing the Plate.*

The book states that,

> "Contemporary American Christians are among the wealthiest of their faith in the world today and probably the most affluent single group of Christians in two thousand years of church history. They have a lot of money.… Most American Christians also profess to want to see the gospel preached in the world, the hungry fed, the Church strengthened, and the poor raised to enjoy lives of dignity and hope — all tasks that normally require money. And yet, despite all of this, American Christians give away relatively little money to religious and other purposes.… Only a small percent of American Christians give money generously, in proportion to what their churches call them to give."[12]

That is the bad news. Now, let's look at the good news. The book continues:

> "We estimate that if committed Christians [who either attend church regularly — a few times a month or more frequently — or profess to be 'strong' or 'very strong'] in the United States gave 10 percent of their after-tax-income — fully but no more than 10 percent — that would provide an extra $46 billion per year of resources with which to fund needs and priorities. That represents nearly an additional 25 percent of what all Americans — Christians or otherwise — currently give in all types of private philanthropy."[13]

I can't imagine $46 billion, but I can imagine how much good could be accomplished with a few million dollars.

Obviously, in this book we are not talking about stewardship and giving in general, but these figures graphically support our assumption that there is vast untapped wealth in the Church. Our goal is to teach you how to harvest some of that wealth.

ADDITIONAL SOURCES OF WEALTH

Some wealthy people set up private or family trusts. The trust funds are invested and the trust makes gifts to various charities. According to Lyle Schaller, "The number of family foundations increased from approximately 30,000 in 1990 to an estimated 48,000 at the end of 2001."[14] You may have an individual or couple in your congregation who has such a trust. You may have a couple whose daughter or son grew up in the Church, who is now an executive of a large corporation, whose income is six or seven figures. Those individuals could be major gift prospects, especially for special projects or memorial gifts.

Some non-members may also be prime prospects. For example, the parents of a kid whose life got turned around because of your, or the church's, interest in him/her. The proud parents of children who attend church school, who have resources, may be prospects.

A couple in town who belong to no church, who have no children, may be good prospects. They may need help in deciding what to do with their assets, their home or the three farms they inherited. You can be very helpful in guiding them.

A word of caution — keep your research and records highly confidential. Don't share them with anyone except your successor. When gathering information on prospects be very discreet. Don't divulge why you are doing it. If your targeted members learn why you are gathering information they might be turned off.

Another way to identify wealth is to get your hands on lists of donors to other projects or capital campaigns. Those might include the new library, the addition to the art center, the new addition to the school, or contributions to public radio or TV. College and university annual reports often list donors in categories of gift amounts. Those lists of donors can provide you clues as to who has wealth and who is generous. Some of them may be members of your parish.

As said before, some wealthy individuals and couples establish trusts. Those are established in banks or financial institutions and gifts are made from them to charitable organizations, including churches. Those trusts are public information and their gift policies are readily available. Libraries, especially larger city libraries, usually have lists of foundations by gift category, policy, state, and other information. Much of the information is also available on the internet.

Ownership of farm land, another source of wealth, is public information. The county clerk in each county in Iowa has a record of the ownership of plots of farm land. I assume that information is available in other states. The local Farm Bureau or County Extension Office can tell you where to obtain a county plat map that lists agricultural land and who owns it.

Additional sources of wealth that often do not show up on the radar screen include the private investors. Those individuals or couples who sold their business, inherited wealth, or have been successful investors. They may show little evidence of wealth. They may have a small office downtown with no sign on the door, or no office at all. Another category that may be overlooked is the owners of six McDonalds, twelve Burger Kings, or three apartment buildings. They also may have a small office in an older building downtown where they go each morning to get their mail and then go and have coffee with their buddies. No evidence, no blip on the financial radar screen, but the wealth is definitely there, and if they are your members, they are prospects. If not, they may become prospects.

One very wealthy former prospect of mine has an office attached to his garage. The office is about the size of a one-car garage. His desk, his secretary's desk, filing cabinets, book shelves, and a couple of folding metal chairs for visitors, are squeezed into the office. The house is average middle-class. The new pickup in the drive didn't tell me much. However, my research indicated that he had a thriving business with a crew of construction people and equipment that built nursing homes. He maintained a crew of construction people year round. I was told that within the past year or so he had purchased several commercial jet air liners, had them refurbished, and leased them back to airlines. The wealth was there but I had to dig to find it. From all appearances he has a very small operation, but he is probably one of the wealthiest men in Iowa. You may have to dig, but the effort may well be worth it.

A fundraiser friend of mine told me this wonderful story. On a Saturday morning a few years ago, a Boy Scout and his dad knocked on the door of a couple in Tucson, Arizona. The husband, whom we'll call Hubert, met them and invited them into the living room to sit down.

The boy, in his Scout uniform, khaki shirt and pants, merit badges, red neckerchief and all, and his dad in Scout-dad attire. They said they were raising money to build a badly needed addition to the dining hall at the Scout camp up in the mountains. After sharing their story, they told Hubert the addition would cost $100,000 and asked him to consider a contribution (the cost would probably be $500,000 today). Hubert went into the kitchen and talked with his wife. After a few minutes he returned and said, "We'll do it."

The mystified father said, "I don't understand. How much will you give?" "We'll give you the $100,000 to build the building," said Hubert. Can you imagine the excitement when the boy and his father returned to the Scout office and reported they had a generous couple who would fund the entire addition? And that isn't the end of the story!

That donor was the son of a man who had built a large lumber and household products business from scratch. The son and his wife inherited huge wealth. That dining hall gift was followed by many additional gifts. The Scout leadership wisely included the couple in events. They were frequent guests of the camp and met many of the boys. The relationship with the camp and the Scouts that began on that Saturday morning lasted many years and was a source of great pleasure and satisfaction to that couple. As we say in the development business, "You never know what you'll get until you ask." In another venue, it says, "Ask and you shall receive."

A final word: a member or members of your congregation or parish may be the very best source of information about who in your flock has wealth. Bankers, stock brokers, lawyers, insurance executives, business men and women, financial advisors, farm managers and wealthy people can be excellent sources of information about wealth or wealthy people.

Approaching them requires some careful diplomacy. Bankers and other professionals are prohibited by law from divulging confidential information about their customers. Be discrete. Up front, with bankers and other professionals, make it clear that you are *not* asking for *confidential information*. You are asking only for *public information* — that is, information that is widely known. In most cases, people will give you public information or refer you to others who have information that will be helpful to you. Non-professionals are not bound by those laws or policies and may be very resourceful and helpful to you.

Large congregations, especially those who have highly-transient constituents, like snow birds, who attend for only a few months each year, may choose to purchase information on their members. There are several companies who will run a list of your members through their databases of wealthy individuals. Their databases are able to identify people by several indicators of wealth: zip code, stock holdings, job title, and many other factors. That data can be very helpful. One such company is WealthEngine at www.wealthid.com or phone number 301.215.5980. For others, consult the web.

(The research form on the next page will help you gather and record vital information on prospects.)

PROSPECT INFORMATION FORM

Date_____

Name(s)_____

Preferred Nickname_____

Address_____ City_____ Zip_____

Telephone_____ Cell Phone_____

Marital Status_____ E-mail_____

Approximate Ages: Male_____ Female_____ Other_____

Vocation(s) or Profession(s)_____

Working?_____ Retired?_____

Children/Ages_____

Influential Family Member(s)_____

Influential Friends/Associates_____

_____

Church Involvement — Past and Present_____

Interests/Avocation(s)_____

_____

Values or Strong Beliefs_____

Estimated Annual Household Income_____

Estimated Total Net Worth_____

Information About Your Resources_____

Giving History to Church and Other Organizations_____

_____

Lawyer/Financial Adviser_____

Person Handling Finances (if any)_____

1   Smith, Christian; Emerson, Michael, *Passing the Plate,* Oxford Press, Oxford, NY, 2008, used by permission of Oxford University Press, Inc., 11

2   Ibid.

3   Ibid., 12

4   Schaller, Lyle E., *The New Context for Ministry,* Abingdon Press, Nashville, TN, 2002, 151

5   Danko, William D., and Thomas, Stanley J., *The Millionaire Next Door,* MJF Books, New York, NY, 1996, used by permission of Taylor Trade Publishing, Lanham, MD, 12

6   Ibid.

7   Ibid., 9–11

8   Schaller, Lyle E., *The New Context for Ministry,* Abingdon Press, Nashville, TN, 186

9   Ibid., 185–186

10   Ibid., 186

11   Ibid.

12   Smith, Christian; Emerson, Michael, *Passing the Plate,* Oxford Press, Oxford, NY, 2008, used by permission of Oxford University Press, Inc., 3

13   Ibid., 13

14   Schaller, Lyle E., *The New Context for Ministry,* Abingdon Press, Nashville, TN, 2002, 159

Chapter Six

Deferred Gifts — The Motherlode

" If you die without making a will, you'll never do it again."
DWIGHT HEINRICHS

*"Making a will doesn't mean you're willing to pass on — to die, that is. But not making a will
doesn't mean you won't. It just means you've messed things up thoroughly for those left behind.
It's all well and good for Howard Hughes to thus devote his countless billions to the welfare
of lawyers. Most of us, however, think the legal profession does quite well enough without
our leaving estates to be consumed in fees while we are probably being consumed in flames."*
MALCOLM FORBES (1977)

Charles O'Malley, now deceased, attended St. Patrick's Catholic Church and School in Perry, Iowa. His mother, Nora O'Malley, had been very active in getting the school started. It was dedicated in 1921. She died the day it was dedicated.

After graduation, Charles went to New York where he eventually graduated from Columbia University. Charles was an entrepreneur and a very successful businessman. At one time he made a contribution of $500,000 to St. Patrick's School.

When he died in 2009, his attorney came to Perry, to meet with Pastor David Polish, and to visit the school. It was at that time that he informed David that Charles had left $4.5 million to St. Patrick's. Yes, $4.5 million — *$300,000 each year for fifteen years!*

We don't know if any pastor of St. Patrick's ever contacted Charles about a gift or not. Charles had some contacts over the years including family weddings and funerals. The point is obvious. A very wealthy man who grew up in the Church — and no doubt, had some wonderful memories of his time there and of his mother's dedication to the Church — decided on his own, to leave a huge deferred trust to the parish. Who knows, there may be such a generous individual out there who grew up in *your* parish, and is a prospect for a major gift.

What the gold rush was to Alaska in the 1890s and to California in 1848, the potential for deferred gifts is to the Church today. There is wealth in the Church. Where there is wealth there is the potential for bequests. However, the very wealthy are not the only prospects for deferred gifts. An unmarried elderly school teacher who owns her own modest $100,000 home and has a retirement fund of $150,000 is a prospect for a major deferred gift. There are exceptions, I'm sure, but the majority of congregations would have a few prospects for deferred gifts. In some congregations, especially those with several hundreds of members, the potential for gifts by will or estate plan is beyond imagination.

What is the potential for deferred gifts to the Church? According to *Giving USA™ 2008*, "Charitable bequests [in 2007] are estimated to be $23.15 billion.... [1] Charitable bequests for 2007 are estimated to be 7.6 percent of the total standard giving."[2]

Those bequests were distributed to many different agencies, including religious organizations. "In 2006, charitable bequests reported by tax refunds totaled $17.54 billion. Bequests designated for 'religions' totaled $1.17 billion."[3]

Considering the wealth that is present in the Church, the "trillion-dollar transfer" of wealth in the United States, and the fact that the population is growing older, it doesn't take an MIT economist to recognize the huge potential for deferred gifts.

(For more information on the potential for deferred gifts to the Church and the giving motivation of people who have bequests in their wills or estate, please see Chapter Seven.)

"In a survey commissioned by *The Non-Profit Times*, more than half of adults polled do not have a will, or if they have a will, have not left money to a charity."[4] A former seminary classmate of mine and a fundraiser in Minnesota, Dwight Henrichs, once shared this quote: "If you ever die without a will, you'll never do it again." How true. If half of your congregation does not have a will, imagine the potential for bequests if they were persuaded to make a will and to leave a bequest of 25 percent or more of their estate to your church!

Who makes a will? Research indicates that first will makers are typically in their 40s. The majority are between 40 and 60. Many people revise their will in their late 60s and 70s. "Only about 15 percent of those who decide to make planned gifts arrive at those decisions when they are 75 or older. By comparison, 17 percent of planned gift donors are younger than 45."[5] By the time most people have achieved age 75, and have made a will, they have decided how their estate will be disbursed.

Just how important is a will? Very important. The law makes it possible for individuals to decide how their assets will be disbursed. Regardless of the size of the estate, the individual can determine to whom or to what cause his/her worldly assets will go. In the absence of a will, or a poorly written will, an individual's disbursement of the property will be dictated by the intestate laws of the state. The state decides to whom or to what cause, if any, the estate will go. The wishes, or intentions, of the individual may be totally ignored. This can lead to disappointment, confusion, anger, and conflict among family members.

By making a will, the donor decides if family members are to be included. Or friends, or causes, including his church. A will can eliminate conflicts and opposing opinions of family members. Through the will the donor can continue his/her influence by contributing to those causes and supporting those values he/she has supported during lifetime. The donor's assets will, through his/her bequests, continue to work for decades to come.

When you encourage your people to make a will you are doing them a big favor. You are also doing their children and grandchildren a big favor. You are also laying the ground work for bequests to your church.

The First Unitarian Church in Des Moines, Iowa, has a very aggressive and effective committee and program to encourage members to make deferred gifts to the Church. My wife and I visited there to see a grandson perform in a program. During the same service, several people who had established a deferred gift were publicly recognized. Their program could be an excellent guide for others. (See the Appendix.)

---

1   *Giving USA™ 2008*, Giving USA Foundation™, Chicago, IL, 56

2   Ibid.

3   Ibid., 60

4   Ibid.

5   Ibid., 66

Chapter Seven

The Real Reasons Why People Give

"In the 'warm glow' of philanthropy, people aren't giving money merely to save the whales; they're also giving to feel the glow that comes with being the kind of person who's helping to save the whales."
JAMES ANDREONI

"Human behavior arises [results] more often from emotional and irrational causes than from logical."
REPORT OF THE AMERICAN INSTITUTE OF MOTIVATION RESEARCH

Why did a couple in Des Moines, Iowa, give over a million dollars to finance the remodeling of First United Methodist Church? Why did the members of Plymouth Congregational Church in Des Moines, contribute millions to construct a large addition to the existing structure? Why did a retired veterinarian in Boone, Iowa, leave in his will bequests of $25,000 to his church and $100,000 to support his denomination's camp and retreat program?

If you, as pastor, priest, or rabbi, know and understand what motivates people to give, you will be much more effective in obtaining major gifts from your congregation. One of the objectives of this book is to help you and other clergy feel more confident and be more successful leading your congregation to adequately and generously provide funding for your programs. As a clergyperson you have great potential to solicit major and deferred gifts and thus, to expand your mission and ministry.

A key question in regard to understanding why people give is, "What is the donor's motivation for making the gift? Why is she doing it?" Does anyone give out of pure altruism? Or, is self-interest always part of the equation? The issue of motivation in giving, or more specifically, the question as to whether giving is motivated by pure altruism or self-interest, is discussed by Dwight Burlingame. He states that, "Altruism is one end of a continuum which is anchored by egoism on the other. Both motives come together in the human condition to form a cooperative venture to achieve nearly all ends in society."[1]

"Altruism," according to Burlingame, "can be defined as unselfish action for the welfare of others or, as the *Oxford English Dictionary* states it, 'devotion to others' or 'regard for others as a principle of action.'"[2]

In *Altruism and Philanthropy*, Burlingame writes, "various religious traditions have led the way through centuries in the promotion of altruism. Christianity emphasizes acts of love or charity to demonstrate one's faith in God."[3]

Burlingame continues, "He [Robert Fogel] further notes that the Judeo-Christian tradition recognizes that altruism and egoism go together. Both the Jewish Torah and the Christian Gospels speak of loving our neighbors as we love ourselves. Self-interest has value as a function of the larger good: the larger good depends upon effective care of the self."[4]

It is impossible to know with certainty another's, and perhaps one's own, motives for giving gifts, but the evidence indicates that altruism and egoism, totally unselfish giving, and self-interest are operative in most giving. Perhaps the most important factor for clergy is to be aware that self-interest, either in a personal sense or in a community sense, often influences the prospective donor's decision.

Carl Rogers and Abraham Maslow, noted psychologists, "... have considered it human nature to help others in distress or to make personal sacrifices for the good of the community. Accordingly, failure to perform such actions represents a distortion of basic human characteristics by negative experience and social inequities."[5]

Dacher Keltner has done a great deal of research on human emotions and their influence on behavior. The results of his research are reported in his significant new book, *Born To Be Good*.[6] Of special interest to us is his work on compassion and sympathy as they relate to altruism. He says that compassion has long been considered a "blind emotion," a soft or even detrimental emotion. However, his research and that of many other reliable researchers indicates quite the opposite.

Keltner argues that compassion emanates from the vagus nerve system in the human body. The vagus system is the source, the motivation for identifying with and responding to the pain, suffering, and need of our fellow humans.

Keltner's conclusion suggests that significant compassion is the motivation for altruistic behavior. He says that humans are "wired" for compassion, for altruism, for giving.

In regard to the influence of the emotions in people's motivation for giving, the late economist, James Andreoni, argued that the influence of the emotions was much more important than generally believed. In order to put a name on that phenomenon, he referred to it as the "warm glow theory." In the "warm glow theory," Andreoni held that when people contributed to saving the whales they were giving as much to being associated with people who were saving the whales as to saving the whales.

A few years ago the American Institute of Motivation Research, in Los Angeles, California, published a paper reporting the results of an extensive study on motivation for giving to the Church. The study provides valuable information as to what motivates church people to give and indicates that people operate on, or respond to, requests for contributions on three separate levels.[7]

The first is the conscious level. On this level, logic and reason are dominant. This might be described as the "intellectual level." The second level is the "preconscious" which the report describes as "vague feelings, sensations — characterized by prejudices, fears and assumptions."[8] These vague influences, the study says, are usually nebulous and difficult to articulate. The researchers describe the third level as the "unconscious or subconscious" level. People are totally unaware of these subconscious influences although they, the feelings, may strongly affect the donor's decisions.

Pastors and others who seek to motivate giving must keep in mind that these three levels determine people's responses. Even when the appeal is "logical," the response is highly influenced by preconscious and subconscious factors. A wise motivator will consider all three levels of influence.

Those who desire to promote giving must also understand a primary finding of the study. That is, "… that human behavior arises (results) more often from emotional and irrational causes than from logical."[9] We are emotional, feeling beings and those who would motivate us will appeal to our emotions, according to the study. A basic drive in all of us is self-preservation in which emotions are deeply involved. That drive causes us to ask, what will this gift do for me? What will I get, or how will I feel, if I contribute to, participate in, or support, this effort?

According to the American Institute study, there are seven "basic motivation factors that influence giving to religious institutions."[10] The factors are listed along with my (the author's) comments about each of them:

1) *Ego-gratification*. The factor of ego-gratification or self-aggrandizement is a most potent factor. As a result of their gift some people feel empowered, important. They are, by making a contribution, especially a large gift, to a certain program or effort, influencing the outcome. They are feeding hungry children or helping build a church in New Orleans. They are, in fact, exercising their power, controlling outcomes, and influencing results. Some of these people will thrive on recognition and praise.

2) *Emotional security*. We humans want and need to feel emotionally secure. We want to be recognized, affirmed, accepted and loved. We also want to be free of fear, the sense of abandonment and loneliness, and of feelings of guilt and inadequacy. By giving to the Church people may enjoy feelings of recognition and belonging, they may become part of the "family." They may also enjoy feelings of affirmation and belonging as members who support the "family." And, since "God loves a cheerful giver," they may have a deep and abiding sense that they are loved by God.

3) *Assuage of guilt feelings*. During our lifetime, according to the study, "we generate certain hostilities and anti-social tendencies. Those come into conflict with our conscious desires to adjust to society."[11] Those latent hostilities are evident in the vicious attacks on blacks and

gays occasionally reported in the news or recorded on video cameras. Or, in the inappropriate verbal attack on black hecklers made by Michael Richards at the comedy club called Laugh Factory, in West Hollywood. I suspect that many, if not most, of us have some subconscious and perhaps conscious feelings of guilt or inadequacy. By giving, we may be able to reduce those feelings of prejudice, anger, guilt or inadequacy.

4) *Narcissism.* Narcissism is defined as, "having a highly inflated ego, strong feelings of self-love, over emphasis on one's value and abilities."[12] These individuals seek identification of themselves in other objects and people reinforcing awareness of themselves — a sort of "self-substantiation." The narcissist in some people causes them to identify in others, qualities that they possess or desire to possess. A young athlete identifies with Michael Phelps, a young, aspiring actress identifies with Sandra Bullock or Julia Roberts. Narcissists may also seek recognition and affirmation that they are important.

5) *Social acceptance.* One of the basic human needs, one that contributes greatly to one's sense of contentment or happiness, is the need for relationships with others, with family, friends and associates. However, the sense of being separate, of being alone in the world, is pervasive in our culture. The lack of meaningful contact, of interaction with others, leads to feelings of isolation and loneliness. To overcome those negative feelings many people seek relationships, to be involved with, recognized by, and accepted by others. We join a church or parish. We support it, and it provides us a sense of belonging. One woman who attends the church that my wife and I attend expressed her feelings of acceptance by the church when she said, "The Church is my family."

6) *Love objects.* People tend to identify in others the qualities that they would like to have in themselves. A teenager idolizes a rock star, or actress, because she would like to have those talents or abilities. To be a star! Adults identify with actors and actresses, philanthropists, leaders, and wealthy or powerful individuals. They wish they could be Donald Trump or Bill Gates and possess wealth, fame and power. Those who wish to promote generosity may be able to use this "need" to their advantage.

7) *Status seeking.* Those who grew up with feelings of inadequacy and inferiority, as I did, can readily understand the search for symbols or relationships that reinforce the ego, the sense of adequacy. Those symbols or relationships help us to have feelings of self-worth, of self-value. The status symbol "is often a crutch for a crippled ego," according to the American Institute study.[13] By supporting the Church, the member validates or publicly declares his or her involvement in the Church. If the Church, in turn, recognizes that person as a valuable member of the congregation, as a "child of God," their sense of being and belonging is reinforced.

My research indicates that donors to churches, synagogues, and other religious organizations are motivated primarily from the following:

1) Church membership or association with the institution. Obviously, those who are affiliated with a given congregation or parish are more likely to contribute to that church and its programs.

2) Regard for the local church. Church members who have a positive attitude toward their parish or synagogue are more likely to support the organization.

3) Being involved in the Church as an adult. People who have participated in the Church and have served on boards and commissions are more likely to make major gifts, if they are able, than those who joined more recently. While raising funds to improve the youth camp sites in the United Methodist Conference in Iowa, I called on clergy, including many retired clergy, all over the state of Iowa. Many of them pledged to the program. Frequently, clergy people would relate their camping experiences as a youth. A substantial number felt their call to ministry as the result of camping experiences. They benefited greatly from their participation in church-sponsored camping and willingly contributed to the camps campaign.

4) Respect for the pastor/priest and other professional leaders. In the years that I served as a program consultant for the Iowa Conference I worked with many churches assisting some of them with financial problems. If the pastor were respected, if he conducted himself in a professional manner, and if he related well to the people, raising funds was a lot easier. If, on the contrary, he was not held in high regard, not well liked or respected, raising money was a challenge.

5) Agreement with the goals and mission of the institution. A bulletin published by the Iowa Health Foundation quotes Henry (Hank) Goldstein, Chair of the Giving USA Foundation™, "People are motivated to give because they value the cause, whether it is religion, education, health care, or international relief…. "[14] It goes without saying that the members of a synagogue or parish believe in the mission of the parish or they would not have joined it. In *A System Approach to Stewardship,* the Center for Parish Development in Chicago states that a parish must build its programs (ministry and mission) on the goals and needs of the members of the parish. *A System Approach to Stewardship* also says, "If my personal goals coincide with the church's goals, then I am increasingly motivated to give my time, energy and money to my church. I see my church as enabling me to achieve my personal goals."[15]

6) A strong interest in, or involvement with, a specific program. The response to Hurricane Katrina that devastated New Orleans and the tragic earthquake in Haiti are good examples. Thousands of people were passionate about both contributing and volunteering to help the victims.

7) Respect for the volunteer leadership of the church or synagogue. Church members tend to respect the volunteer leaders of their congregations. They say to themselves, "John, who is a member of the official board of our church, is a good man. I trust him to make good decisions for the Church."

8) Involvement in a campaign to raise funds for a specific program. If people get involved in a program or cause, they are more likely to contribute to it. People who serve on the administrative board, the finance committee or the building committee are strongly motivated to contribute to a program when they have been involved in the planning. They have developed ownership. Ownership supports generosity.

9) Confidence in the state, national and international leadership and mission of the denomination. In order to take full advantage of this motivator the leadership of a congregation or denomination must make every effort to provide feedback about the accomplishments of state, regional and national programs funded by the Church or the denomination. They must make that information available to the congregation. If people are aware of what the denomination is doing in state, national and international programs, they are more likely to support the programs.

In addition to the above, I want to suggest these additional factors that I have found motivate people to give. The first motivator may relate to several of the above but I think it is worth mentioning. It is *the use of contributions as instruments of power.* By giving to certain causes, organizations, or programs, people can, to some extent, control circumstances, goals and outcomes. A basic human need is to feel important; that we are making a difference in the world. By emphasizing how a gift will result in bringing about a positive or desired change, a priest, rabbi, or pastor will be applying this effective motivator. The flip side of this factor is that disgruntled or unhappy church members may exercise their influence and power by withholding their gifts.

This additional motivator is, *a sense of appreciation, of gratitude.* Many years ago, a Canadian student, Murray Wise, applied to Iowa State University (ISU). He had not graduated high school. Because of that, he was turned down by some other colleges and universities. ISU accepted him on probation. He worked hard and was an excellent student. In a few years, he became a very successful real estate broker.

Many years later, when I met with him at his palatial new home in Florida, he expressed deep gratitude to ISU because the university accepted him. He felt that the faculty set him on a path to success and wealth. As an expression of his gratitude, his goal was to establish a $1 million scholarship program at ISU. His primary motivation was gratitude. We were discussing the details of the scholarship when I retired from the University.

Appreciation. You and I are the recipients of life, health, family, home, meaningful work, security, and opportunity in this great land. All of this from the Creator! God and Life have poured out this bounty upon us. What a powerful reason for supporting the Church.

The final motivator I want to suggest is *the desire to be identified with others who are supporting a program or organization.* As has been suggested earlier in this chapter, donors may be motivated more by being affiliated with others who are helping to save the whales than by interest in saving the whales.

A review of recent research into motivation for giving will help us. A 2007 study of philanthropy, sponsored by the Bank of America,[16] provides us some very important, reliable, and current research on why people in "high net-worth" households give. This study reflects the opinions of nearly 1,400 respondents throughout the United States with household income greater than $200,000 and/or net-worth [excluding the value of their residence] of at least $1,000,000.[17]

Although it is reasonable to believe that the percentage of "high net-worth" people who are participating in churches and synagogues is relatively small, it is also reasonable to assume that some of them are active in their church. A review of the factors that motivate them to contribute will provide us a better understanding of their motivations and perhaps help us to understand the motives of members with average resources as well.

The *Bank of America Study of High Net-Worth Philanthropy: Portraits of Donors* (2007), divides donors into three categories that are of particular interest to us. They are 1) the very wealthy, 2) the devout, and 3) the bequeathers. The "very wealthy" are those with a net-worth of more than $50 million. The "devout" are those who attend a church, temple or synagogue once per week or more and donate to religious causes. The "bequeathers" are those households who have made provisions in their wills to leave 25 percent or more of their estate to charity.

The very wealthy respondents identified the following *factors* that caused them to give to charity (the figures indicate the percentage of the respondents who checked that motivator):

Meet critical needs (86%)
Those with more should share with those with less (69%)
Giving back to society (85.7%)
Bring about a desired impact (72.1%)
Religious beliefs (46.5%)
Non-profits should provide services when government cannot (61.9%)
Set an example (69.8%)
Being asked (61.9%)
Identifying with causes (53.5%)[18]

According to the Bank of America study, "… the very wealthy were more concerned [than other wealthy respondents] about their ability to determine the impact of their gifts and about the mission and goals of non-profits."[19]

"Seventy-six point two (76.2%) percent of the very wealthy said they would give more to charities if 'less money [were] spent on administration and fundraising,' and sixty-six point seven (66.7%) percent said they would give more if they were 'able to determine the impact of gifts.'"[20]

The obvious message to churches and religious organizations is *one,* to be clear about the goals and mission of the organization, and *two,* to clearly communicate the goals and mission and to provide feedback on how and to what extent those goals have been achieved.

Additionally, of particular interest to churches and denominations is the fact that approximately forty percent (40%) of the wealthy respondents said they would give more to charity if they were 'able to volunteer skills in non-profits.'"[21] What church, synagogue, or denomination could not benefit from the service of additional, wealthy volunteers?

The "bequeather" is another category of the households analyzed in the Bank of America Study, that are of particular interest to churches. The bequeathers have a provision in their wills to leave 25 percent or more of their estate to charity.

According to the Bank of America Study, "They [the bequeathers] give statistically significantly more to charity than non-bequeathing households. In fact, they give about four and a half times as much to charity. Bequeathing households have statistically significantly more income and wealth and were much more likely to report feeling financially secure than other high net-worth households.... Bequeathing households are likely to be between 61 and 70 years of age. Over half live in the Northeast and Great Lakes region of the United States.... Bequeathing households are also much more likely to be childless than other wealthy households, 33.3 and 8.5 percent respectively."[22] The bequeathers in this study gave a mean of $525,418 to charity in 2005 and a mean of $80,891 to religious causes, while the high net-worth households gave a mean of $120,651 to charity and a mean of only $20,530 to religious causes.[23]

"Approximately eighty-six percent (86%) of the bequeathers listed *Giving back to society* as a major motivator for their giving. They listed *Meeting critical needs* (81.5%), *Those with more should help those with less* (81.5%), *Bring about a desired impact* (76.5%), and *Religious beliefs* (54.8%)."[24]

According to *Giving USA™ 2008*, bequests by will to charities in 2006 amounted to an estimated $17.44 billion, compared with the $199 billion given by living individuals.[25]

The Bank of America study did not indicate whether the study asked how many of the respondents did not have a will. That would be interesting. The study did state that "... approximately 56 percent of wealthy donors today have a charitable provision in their will — a total that could climb to a staggering 93 percent in 2010, because an additional 37 percent of donors would consider establishing a charitable provision in their wills in the next three years."[26]

The *Bequest Giving Study for Campbell and Company* (published in March of 2007), conducted by the Center on Philanthropy of Indiana University, analyzed data "from more than 2,000 household surveys conducted in four states or regions to assess the differences in characteristics between those who have a charity in their wills and those who would consider adding a charity to their wills."[27] The data was compared with the Bank of America study of 1,400 "high net-worth" households.[28]

The Campbell and Company study states that "only a small minority of households (8%), report leaving a charitable bequest in their wills (National Council on Planned Giving). In principle, anyone who gives during his/her lifetime is a potential bequest donor."[29] Their data supports my earlier assertion that the potential for cultivating deferred gifts to the Church, synagogue, cathedral, or denomination is "off the charts."

The Campbell and Company study also indicates that the age of people who have named a charity in their will ranges from 40–60 years. Baby boomers, ages 40–60, represent a "significant share of those who have already named a charitable gift in their will and also those who are willing to consider making a bequest (50% and 51% respectively)."[30]

According to the Campbell and Company Study, those who have graduate-level degrees comprised the largest percentage of people who have a charity in their will. Although individuals with bachelor's degrees represent a much larger segment of the respondents, only nine percent of those studied currently have a charity in their will. "Income was not found to affect the likelihood that a donor would bequest or consider the bequest of a charitable gift in his/her will."[31] This indicates that in an average congregation one-fourth to one-third of the congregants are prospects for a planned gift! The potential for planned gifts to religious institutions is astronomical!

Of special interest to religious leaders, here, is that people ages 40–70 who have household income between $50,000 and $75,000 and retirees with income between $25,000 and $50,000 are also prime prospects for planned gifts to the Church.

The third category of wealthy donors included in the Bank of America Study is the "devout," those households who attend a church or religious organization once or more per week. Keep in mind that they are also high net-worth households.

The "… devout households give less on average to secular causes ($68,892) than other high net-worth households ($102,553), but 50 percent more on average to religious organizations ($31,179) compared with $20,530, respectively."[32] The report continues, "However, the median gift donated to charity by devout households was 40 percent more than other high net-worth households ($23,500 and $16,500, respectively) and more than double the amount donated by secular households ($23,500 and $10,000, respectively) suggesting that the devout tended to have a smaller range and variation in giving than did all other high net-worth households.[33]

"*Religious beliefs* were ranked highest among their [the devout's] reasons for giving (98.7%), while *Those with more should help those with less* (86.4%), *Meet critical needs* (85.9%), *Giving back to society* (83.4%), *Bring about a desired impact* (69.7%), and *Non-profits should provide services that government can't* (69.4%), were ranked in descending order. Sixty-one point seven percent (61.7%) listed *Being asked* as a major motivator. Forty-three percent (43%) of devout households said they would give more if they were 'able to use their skills in non-profits.'"[34] "Devout households said they would give more to charity if 'less money were spent on administration' (77.2%), [they were] 'able to determine impact of gifts' (63.2%), and 'able to volunteer skills in non-profits' (43%)."[35]

In his book, *Giving and Stewardship in an Effective Church*, Kennon Callahan makes an important point. That is that pastors and others who would motivate giving, need to recognize that what motivates them may not be what motivates the members of their congregations. If a pastor emphasizes compassion only, he/she may fail to relate to the rational, intellectual types in his/her congregation. A wise pastor or leader will, over time, emphasize a variety of motivational influences.[36]

In summary, the pastor, priest, rabbi or denominational executive who wishes to increase giving and cultivate donors of major and deferred gifts will:

1) Emphasize the religious and biblical teachings about giving, caring for others, Christian stewardship, and related topics.

2) Teach that those who have much have an obligation to help those who have little.

3) Lift up critical needs, the jobless, the homeless, those with no medical insurance, the physically and mentally ill, and the victims of floods, hurricanes, and other catastrophic events.

4) Teach the value of gratitude, of appreciation for the myriad ways that we have been blessed, and that we have an obligation to "give back" to provide those benefits to others.

5) Preach and teach about how a person's giving, their generosity, brings about personal physical, emotional, and spiritual benefits.

6) Provide feedback that indicates the results of the gifts. Tell the people what their gifts have accomplished.

7) Lift up causes, efforts and organizations that are fostering justice, meeting human needs or responding to catastrophic events.

8) Humanize individuals and groups of destitute, homeless and the underserved by visiting shelters and other service organizations and having guest representatives of those under-served groups visit your parish and speak to your people.

9) Keep the costs of administration, including fundraising, at a minimum and maximize the portion of the gifts that go to accomplish goals and mission.

10) Ask for gifts. Many organizations are out there asking for the gifts and getting them! The Church deserves to get its share of the charitable dollar. Ask for the gift. This is the time for courage and decisive action.

11) Involve as many of your wealthy members as possible in volunteer services, and as members of boards, commissions, committees and ad-hoc advocacy groups.

12) Be absolutely transparent with all church finances, income and expenditures, and make regular reports of the same.

13) Find ways to recognize individuals and to praise your people for their generous giving.

These topics can be applied in dozens of ways through preaching, teaching, seminars, newsletter articles, individual conversations, guest speakers, and through written proposals. Use your own creativity and imagination to apply them to major gift work or, for that matter, to promote generosity in giving to your church, synagogue or temple. Others are doing it and you can do it.

1   Burlingame, Dwight F., *Altruism and Philanthropy*, Center on Philanthropy, Indiana University, Indianapolis, IN, 1998, 1

2   *Oxford English Dictionary*, Oxford University Press, s.v. "Altruism," quoted in Burlingame, Dwight F., *Altruism and Philanthropy*, Center on Philanthropy, Indiana University, Indianapolis, IN, 1998, 1

3   Burlingame, Dwight F., *Altruism and Philanthropy*, Center on Philanthropy, Indiana University, Indianapolis, IN, 1998, 1

4   Ibid.

5   Ibid., 2

6   Keltner, Dacher, *Born To Be Good*, W. W. Norton & Company, Inc, New York and London, January 2009, 239–240

7   *Analysis of Problems of Inadequate Church Income Based on Motivation Research*, American Institute of Motivation Research, Los Angeles, CA, Date Unknown

8   Ibid., 1

9   Ibid., 2

10 Ibid., 2–5

11 Ibid., 3

12 Ibid., 4

13 Ibid.

14 Press release from a quote by Henry (Hank) Goldstein, Chair of Giving USA Foundation™, published by AAFRC, a division of the American Association of Fund Raising Counsel, July 8, 2004

15 Ellzey, Charles H. and Dietterich, Paul, *A System Approach to Stewardship*, Center for Parish Development, Module 4, Volume 4 and 5, Chicago, IL, May, 1976

16 *Bank of America Study of High Net-Worth Philanthropy: Portraits of Donors*, Center on Philanthropy, Indiana University, Indianapolis, IN, December 2007

17 Ibid.

18 Ibid., 14

19 Ibid., 15

20 Ibid., 16

21 Ibid.

22 Ibid., 21

23 Ibid.

24 Ibid.

25   *Giving USA™ 2008,* Giving USA Foundation™, Chicago, IL, 2008

26   Ibid., 8

27   *Executive Summary: Bequest Giving Study for Campbell and Company,* Center on Philanthropy, Indiana University, Indianapolis, IN, 2007, 1

28   Ibid.

29   Ibid.

30   Ibid., 2

31   Ibid., 3

32   *Bank of America Study of High Net-Worth Philanthropy: Portraits of Donors,* Center on Philanthropy, Indiana University, Indianapolis, IN, December 2007, 35

33   Ibid.

34   Ibid., 45

35   Ibid., 47

36   Callahan, Kennon, *Giving and Stewardship in an Effective Church,* Jossey-Bass, San Francisco, CA, 1997, Reprinted with permission of John Wiley and Sons, Inc.

Chapter Eight

Persuasion — The Art of Getting the Major Gift

"We cannot emphasize too strongly or stress too much that human behavior is not understandable in ordinary common sense terms — certainly not as it relates to the question of why people give." REPORT OF AMERICAN INSTITUTE OF MOTIVATIONAL RESEARCH

"Persuasion is the ability to induce beliefs and values in other people by influencing their thoughts and actions through specific strategies." KEVIN HOGAN[1]

Would you like to feel more comfortable and confident in presenting your point of view? Would you like to be more persuasive from the pulpit? Would you like to know that you persuaded a wealthy couple to leave your church a large endowment gift? Would you like your congregation to over-pledge the budget by ten percent each year for the next five years? By developing your skills of persuasion you may be able to accomplish these and many other worthy objectives.

We use the skills of persuasion every day. We try to persuade our children to study harder and practice more on the piano. We try to persuade our spouse to be more understanding, attentive and affectionate. We try to persuade our city councilman or a state representative to vote for our chosen legislation.

As pastors we try to persuade our congregation to be more faithful in attending worship. We try to persuade people to teach Church School, to be more generous, to be more loving, and to do more for others. We are using our skills of persuasion all the time. Some of us are fairly skilled in the art. However, bringing an individual or a couple to the point that they agree to contribute $10,000 or $100,000 to a project will probably require a higher level of expertise than most of us have achieved. This chapter will teach you how to develop and apply those higher level skills.

"Persuasion is the ability to induce beliefs and values in other people by influencing their thoughts and actions through specific strategies," according to Kevin Hogan.[2] Put another way, persuasion is the process of using your skills to get people to willingly do what you want them to do, or what you think they should do. Isn't that one of the basic functions of ministry?

The Bible is full of stories of people who had mastered the art of persuasion. A prime example is the apostle Paul, whose persuasive message convinced millions to follow a Man whom they never saw or met. Moses used powerful skills in persuading the Israelites to leave Egypt. Can't you hear the Israelites exclaiming, "You want us to leave and go where? Come on, Moses — get real!"

Current history is replete with people who were, or are masters of persuasion, including, Martin Luther King, Jr., Norman Vincent Peale, Winston Churchill, John Kennedy, John Wesley, Ronald Reagan, Billy Graham, Bill Clinton, Barack Obama, and many others. Most of the U.S. presidents have been powerful persuaders. The leaders of all the world's great religions have been master persuaders. We may not agree with their theology, their tactics, or their extravagant life styles, but many TV evangelists are highly effective at persuading people to accept their beliefs and values. They are also effective in persuading people to send them money — big money! — as recent investigations of several TV evangelists by Senator Charles Grassley of Iowa have revealed.

The exercise of the skills of persuasion by leaders in education, politics, business, commerce, and religion has literally, sometimes dramatically, changed the course of history. Philosophers, religious leaders, poets, national leaders, politicians, educators, and activists have possessed the ability to persuade people, often with dramatic results.

The skills of persuasion are to the clergy and religious leaders what the shiny, stainless-steel tools are to the orthopedic surgeon when he is replacing a knee or a broken hip joint. They are to the clergy what the paint, brush and canvas are to a Michelangelo or a Salvador Dali.

Perhaps this is a good place to say that the skills of persuasion are neither good nor bad, they are neutral. They may be used by saints and humanitarians to raise funds for refugees in Darfur or the victims of Katrina. Or, they may be used by white-collar crooks like Jack Abramoff, the lobbyist who went to jail for persuading Indian tribes to give him millions of dollars to lobby for them in Washington. Hitler used powerful skills of persuasion to influence millions to do heinous things. The difference is one's values, and one's code of ethics and morality. One's values — one's sense of what is right and good — will determine how he/she uses the skills. We have no doubt that clergy and others for whom this book is written, who seek to raise funds for religious, honorable and humanitarian purposes will use the skills accordingly.

Kevin Hogan, whom I referred to earlier, has written a great book, *The Psychology of Persuasion*,[3] which I highly recommend. In the book, he lists what he calls the "Laws of Persuasion." Following, is a list of those "laws" and my comments on each. Knowing these "laws" or principles will help you become a more skilled and effective persuader.

1) *"Law of Reciprocity"* — This law says that if someone gives you something of value you feel obligated to give them something. My friend, Bud Beach, has a snow blower. Bud and my neighbor, Deiter Lichtenberger, are buddies. Often, when we have a heavy

snow, Bud comes and cleans my neighbor's drive and sidewalks and comes over and cleans mine. I never ask him to do it and he resists taking money. But I appreciate the act and insist that he take money. He does something for me and I feel obligated to do something for him. The law of reciprocity.

2) *"Law of Contrast"* — Telemarketers use this law effectively. They may ask you to contribute $200 to the Republican Party, but say that the average gift is $100. You make a pledge of $100 thinking you got off easy. At Iowa State University if a donor had committed $25,000 to a project, I sometimes told another prospect that a generous donor had pledged $25,000. The $10,000 that I was asking the prospect to consider was much smaller and seemed more doable. A contrast could be made between the old social hall that is about to collapse and the proposed new social hall. A related strategy is that of comparison. You might compare the huge missions budget of a sister congregation with the meager missions budget of your congregation.

3) *"Law of Friends"*— This law says that when a friend asks you to do something you are much more likely to do it than if a non-friend asks you. When a friend asks you to do something, you don't want to disappoint the friend and jeopardize the friendship, so you do it. You are also more likely to trust your friend. One sure way of expressing friendship, love, or good will is by doing what you know the friend or beloved wants done.

4) *"Law of Expectancy"* — When someone important to you — a professor, a district superintendent, a bishop, or a valued neighbor — asks you to do something you are more likely to give it a try. My teenage granddaughter, Kevalin, a budding young violinist, was in a youth orchestra in the Twin Cities in Minnesota. Knowing that I spent 20+ years in fundraising, the director of the orchestra asked if I would consult with her and their development officer about the development program of the orchestra. How could I say no?

5) *"Law of Association"* — We tend to support products or ideas that are endorsed by people whom we respect or like. Tiger Woods has been featured in several commercials. William Shatner, from *Star Trek* prominence, sells us Priceline. Michael Phelps represents several products. Politicians seek movie stars and highly-visible entertainers to appear with them. Barack Obama made national headlines when Oprah Winfrey appeared with him and gave him a strong endorsement in Des Moines, Iowa, and in South Carolina.

6) *"Law of Consistency"* — When a person states publicly that he/she believes in a certain way, he/she is likely to hold that position even if it is later proven to be false or questionable. People want to be right, correct, on the right side of the debate. Once they have stated a position they are likely to hold tenaciously to that position.

7) *"Law of Scarcity"* — When I was writing this chapter, Iowa Public Television was conducting their "Festival," their annual fundraising campaign. They frequently said, "There are only a few of these rare and beautiful glass bowls left. You need to rush to the phone and pledge or you will miss out." Right now! Car sales are often limited to a certain date. In persuading people it is often useful to create a sense of urgency. "We need to report your pledge to the building committee on Friday."

8) *"Law of Conformity"* — This might be called the "herd effect." People tend to agree with the thoughts, opinions or beliefs that are held by the majority of people. That

is especially true if the people are respected or considered important. In persuading your congregation to finance your new plan or program, first, persuade a few of your highly-respected members to publicly support the project. Others are likely to follow.

9) *"Law of Power"* — People who are in positions of authority, like college professors, wealthy individuals, congressmen, executives, doctors, and bishops, are perceived to have power or authority, and many of them do. Their behavior and opinions will have a strong influence on others in the congregation. An adaptation of this strategy is to discretely plant the idea of a project or program that you want to move forward, in the minds of one or two of your highly-respected and influential leaders. It becomes their idea and they run with your baton.[4]

I want to add a "law" to Hogan's list. This may be a strategy rather than a "law" but it is worth mentioning. That is, *the strategy of ownership*. This strategy says that if a person or persons are involved in the planning and design of a project, they tend to develop a sense of "ownership" and are more likely to work for it and contribute to it.

Seeking Pleasure — Avoiding Pain

Psychologists tell us that all people seek pleasure, happiness, safety, financial security, a sense of belonging, health, comfort, and love. They also say that people attempt to avoid pain, discomfort, illness, loneliness, fear, worry, anxiety, and physical need. In persuading a person to make a major contribution, it is important to clarify for yourself what the gift will do for that prospect. Ask yourself, "How will she feel as a result of making this gift? Will she be happy that she made this contribution? Will he feel good because his deceased wife talked about a rose garden on the Church lawn before she died?" "Will the Butterfields feel important and powerful in making this major lead gift?" You need to have a clear vision of what *you* want out of this gift, but you also need to be clear about what *your client wants, needs or will enjoy* as a result of the gift. Remember, people are highly influenced by their emotional responses to requests for contributions. The ultimate goal is a win-win approach in which the donor feels fulfilled and gratified about making the gift and you and your parish feel good about the gift.

Understanding and Taking Advantage of People's Psychological Behavior

As discussed in Chapter Seven, psychologists also tell us that in making decisions people operate on three different levels. One is the conscious level, characterized by logic and rationality. The second is the preconscious level which includes vague feelings, sensations and emotions. The third level is the unconscious or subconscious. In the third level, thoughts and feelings are repressed and, except under special circumstances like hypnosis, are not consciously available to us.

Some research indicates that decisions to contribute or not are often determined more by one's feelings (preconscious and unconscious) than by logic. Of course, every proposal must be logical and rational. However, any appeal to one's generosity, must consider all three levels. If the subconscious or unconscious impressions are contrary to the rational appeal, the prospect is not likely to respond positively and make the gift.

The strong message for those who seek to raise major gifts is that one's behavior is determined in large part by one's emotions or feeling experiences. Effective persuaders in politics, religion and business have known this and have for centuries appealed to people's fears, frustrations, hopes and dreams. Again, President George W. Bush aroused the public's fear by insisting that Sadam Hussein had weapons of mass destruction and was harboring terrorists, who were a threat to the United States.

In a report of their research on the motivation for giving, the American Institute of Motivation Research, concludes, "We cannot emphasize too strongly or stress too much that human behavior is not understandable in ordinary common sense terms- certainly not as it relates to the question of why people give. Those who are concerned with the development of effective methods [for promoting generosity] must reorient their thinking along new lines. While individuals respond to rational pleas, the underlying motivational forces are non-rational. They are deep-seated and hidden emotional reasons."[5] Effective persuaders know that people are more likely to respond to proposals for gifts that will result in them feeling valued, appreciated, honored, included, fulfilled, satisfied, proud or powerful.

Kevin Hogan proceeds to present a model for advertising a product and persuading a prospect to purchase an item. This model, below, will serve as a guide for persuading a prospect to make a major gift.

A) What you presently have, who you presently are, or how you presently feel is not satisfactory. *You can do, have, or be more and feel better.*

B) Product/service helps many *people just like you* get that result. [In our terminology, many people have already contributed to this project. They feel good that this ministry to children will be continued for many years.]

C) Try it once. You have nothing to lose *and everything to gain.*

D) Other people will respect you and value you more for using this product/service [for making this lead gift, or leaving your estate to First Church.]

E) *Imagine* your future as you deserve it to be. You can *reach your dreams* and achieve your goals if you use this product/service. [If you make this gift and, as a result, cause these victims to get the justice they deserve, you will have achieved an admirable goal.]

F) This product/service is guaranteed so you can feel secure in making a decision *now.* [Our program/project has been approved by the board and the district superintendent. You can feel secure about that. And, by making this pledge now, you will inspire others to make a contribution.][6]

I think it's appropriate to add another item to the list: By making this major gift you will become a role model of responsible stewardship and generosity to your congregation and to your children and grandchildren. You will also be leading the way for others to give a major gift or bequest to your church.

In Chapter Seven, *The Real Reasons Why People Give*, the motivations or reasons why high net-worth households make contributions to their religious organizations are listed. The reasons why those who have included charities in their wills are also listed. A very effective way to persuade people to make major or planned gifts is to review those motives and to design your proposal to appeal to those basic motives.

It is not likely that one would use all or a majority of those items in one proposal or presentation, but they are considered to be highly-effective factors in persuading people to take the big step.

The following five guidelines — five steps to effective persuasion — will help you to develop a plan and successful strategy for obtaining major and deferred gifts.

Step 1: Develop a well-thought-out plan. What is the need? What is causing the need? What do you wish to accomplish? A program, a building, an endowment fund? Articulate the need and describe the project or program that will solve the problem or need. Prepare photographs, charts, or other supporting materials. Has the decision-making or policy-making board or body of the Church approved the project? How will the gift solve the problem? Is a timeline or target date involved? How will the project benefit the congregation or client group to be served? (Refer to Chapter Nine, *Preparing For and Making a Successful Call.*)

Step 2: Do you know the interests, values and involvement of your prospect? Has she indicated an interest in this type of program? Has she been involved with planning for and discussion about the project and, thus, is informed about the project? Does she appear to have the resources to make the level of gift you are proposing?

Step 3: Develop a strong, rational and emotional case for the proposed project. How will the prospect feel as a result of making the gift? Who are the people who will be fed, educated, served, or empowered as a result of the gift? How will justice be served? Will this gift inspire others to contribute? The prospect may never put the question this bluntly, but it will probably be lurking in the back of his or her mind, "What's in this for me? What will I get in return for the gift?" Be prepared to answer those questions.

Step 4: How will you appeal to the prospect's emotions? Will the program help recruit young people for Christ and the Church (as in the case of church-camping experiences)? Will elderly people be served by the project? Will homeless people be housed and fed? Will the purchase of mosquito nets save the lives of thousands of children in Africa? Will you place the name of her beloved, deceased husband on the project? How will she feel as a result of making the gift?

Step 5: Anticipate questions and objections. What questions are likely to be asked by the prospect? Prepare to answer those questions. Also, anticipate possible objections and prepare a response to each.

Remember, you may be the right person at the right time to appeal to this prospect(s). You have done a good job of preparing for the call. You will do a good job of presenting your case. You can do it!

------

1   Hogan, Kevin, *The Psychology of Persuasion*, Pelican Publishing Company, Gretna, LA, 2004, Used by permission of the publisher, Pelican Press, Company, Inc., 20

2   Ibid.

3   Ibid., 42

3   Ibid., 22

5   *Analysis of the Problem of Inadequate Church Income Based on Motivation Research,* American Institute of Motivational Research, Los Angeles, CA

6   Hogan, Kevin, *The Psychology of Persuasion*, Pelican Publishing Company, Gretna, LA, 2004, Used by permission of the publisher, Pelican Press, Company, Inc., 133

Chapter Nine

Preparing For and Making a Successful Call

Congratulations! You've read this far. You've given a lot of thought to the issue of harvesting major gifts for your parish. You understand that you have a unique opportunity to enhance the financial resources for your congregation or denomination, its mission and ministry.

Let's assume that for several months you have been gathering data on your prospects' personalities, values, church involvement, gift history, including major gifts given to other charities, and their financial resources. You have kept a record of that vital information. You have cultivated this prospect(s) for some time and involved him/them in several ways in the life of the Church. You have a sense that the time is right to present a proposal. (Be sure to read Chapter Seven, *The Real Reasons Why People Give,* and Chapter Eight, *Persuasion — The Art of Getting the Major Gift,* and refer to the Proposal Guide on page 83.) You have given consideration to your timing. (Their daughter's wedding is coming up soon, in San Francisco. Better delay until they get back. Or, if they will be leaving for Tucson after Thanksgiving, you better make an appointment soon.)

Prepare a Compelling Proposal

Your next step is to prepare a proposal. Again, refer to the Proposal Guide on page 83. Also refer to the five steps to effective persuasion on page 73. Tailor the proposal to the interests of the prospect(s). Address it to him/them.

State why you are appealing to him/her. Refer to her years of working with youth, or of service on the missions committee. Describe the need. Explain the solution to the problem. Tell the prospect how this program is unique, how it serves a special purpose.

State the request for the funds. How much money are you asking for? A cash gift or a pledge over one, two, or three years? Is this a "lead" gift that will challenge others? Finally, describe the benefits the donors will derive from making the gift. "You will be helping to provide a new program for the youth of the community, especially those from disadvantaged homes."

Thank the prospects for considering the request.

Have the proposal signed by two heavy hitters, i.e., the pastor and the Chair of the Finance Committee, or the Chair of the Building Committee.

Attach any budgets, charts, or other descriptive materials.

The proposal should be brief, no more than one and a half pages. Put it in an attractive folder. Make it as professional as you can. *This is an extremely important document!*

An Important Issue or Two

Some people are squeamish about asking for a gift. The proposal does the asking if you are reluctant to do so. Keep in mind that successful fundraisers ask for gifts of a specific amount — "the ask." Wealthy people are accustomed to being asked and being presented with a proposal. In the Bank of America study referred to elsewhere in this book a high percentage of respondents said they contributed "because they were asked."

When you ask for a specific amount it conveys the impression that you and the board or the committee have given serious thought to the amount needed and the number of potential donors that have been identified. It indicates that you have done your homework. The ask wasn't pulled out of a hat somewhere.

For example, let's say that the fire marshal says that the furnace needs to be replaced along with the wiring in the sanctuary. The cost estimate is $100,000. You have identified eight (8) or nine (9) potential donors. You plan to ask three (3) prospects for $25,000 each.

You believe at least one (1) of them will contribute $25,000. You hope that the other two (2) will give at least $15,000 each. You have five (5) or six (6) prospects for the remaining balance of $45,000. You plan to ask each of the remaining prospects to give $10,000 each, hoping that three (3) will give $10,000 and two (2) or three (3) will give $5,000 each. Some may exceed your expectations but this plan will probably achieve the goal. If you do not achieve the goal of $100,000 — identify a few prospects for $1,000 to $2,500 to complete the job. You can do it!

Call and make an appointment.

You have a decision to make. Will you invite your prospects to coffee, lunch or dinner? Or will you go to their home? An appointment at their home is the safest. In their home you are not likely to be interrupted. A meal in a restaurant usually involves more time and more conversation. Restaurants can be noisy and friends may drop by to chat, interrupting your presentation. I usually allow about 45 minutes to get settled, to engage in small talk, to make the case, and then to excuse myself. You can always stay longer if the prospect's interest or the circumstance requires an adjustment. Sometimes the prospects want to continue the conversation. However, it is usually wise to excuse yourself soon after you have made your case and presented your proposal.

Prepare yourself for the call.

Athletes and sales people often prepare themselves for a race or an occasion where their performance is crucial, by visioning themselves running the race and crossing the finish line first. Sales people envision themselves closing the sale. You might take a few minutes prior to the call to prepare yourself. In your mind or in meditation, see yourself doing a great job of presenting the case. In your mind's eye see the prospect(s) agreeing to make the gift. Say a prayer for yourself and ask for guidance and support.

This is an important call and you should look your best. Dress accordingly.

You're in the house. They have coffee and snacks ready. They suggest that you gather around the kitchen table. You thank them for taking the time to see you and for their hospitality. A sincere comment or compliment on the beautiful fireplace, the family photos, or the art work from India may help them to feel more comfortable. Or "How is your mother adjusting to her retirement?" Don't get involved in a long discussion. Keep focused on your mission. Keep in mind that they suspect that you are going to ask them to do something. They know about the proposed project being discussed by the administrative board.

Move to the case, the story. "Howard and Kristin, I want to visit with you about the proposed remodeling project…. " (Use any drawings, photographs or other descriptive materials. Don't present the written proposal until you have presented the case verbally, and have answered any questions they have.)

Now, present the proposal. Explain, "I would like you to consider this proposal and to pray about it." If they begin to read or review the proposal, wait quietly until they finish. "I will come back in a few days to see what you've decided. When would be a convenient time for me to call back?"

If your custom is to offer a brief prayer when you make a call in the home, you may want to express thanks for Howard and Kristin's faithfulness to Christ and the Church.

Parenthetically, you need to have a pledge card ready, *but keep it in your folder or brief case out of sight; do not leave it with them!* When you leave the card you lose control. Keep the card until you return to get their decision or until they have agreed to make the gift and are ready to sign it.

You have made your case. You have answered their questions. You have presented the proposal and agreed on a time to return. Now, say good-bye and leave.

When you get back to your office or, no later than the next day, write a simple "thank you" note to them and put it in the mail.

A few thoughts to keep in mind regarding the call: Choose your seating arrangement to your advantage. If your prospects are a couple, sit across from the two of them at the table or in the living room. If you sit between them or approximately between them you have to direct your conversation back and forth like a ping pong game. If you are seated directly across from both of them you can direct your conversation to both. I prefer the kitchen or dining room table.

Keep in mind, this is not a "social call." Your objective is to present your cause and to persuade these folks to make a contribution. Like many of my clergy friends, I tend to talk too much. I have consciously worked to reign in my verbosity and to focus when making a call. Some of us tend to talk when we're nervous or unsure — watch yourself. Follow the KIBS approach: "Keep It Brief, Stupid."

If meeting with a couple, be sure to direct your conversation to her as well as to him. Some males tend to direct conversations to other males. That is especially true of older, 60+ males. Older male prospects are more likely to be the decision-makers but in some cases the wife is the decision maker. Even if she is quiet and says very little, she has at least one vote for your proposal, and she may be the one who makes the decision. Be sure to include her. Direct questions and comments to her, as well as to him.

A year or so ago, good friends of mine were called on by a development officer from St. Paul's Theological Seminary in Kansas City. The inept fundraiser obviously directed his conversation to the husband. The wife is a sensitive, intelligent, savvy, professional woman. She was very conscious of his behavior and was offended. To the seminary's detriment, the fundraiser was out of touch with feminist reality.

In support of your case, you may want to remind your prospects that the Building Committee proposed the project and the Official Board approved the project. Mention names of respected members of those groups. Assure your clients that your meeting and discussion of the issues will be kept in strict confidence. What they decide will be kept between you and them. And, keep that trust.

If they seem to hesitate, ask what concerns them. If it's the amount proposed, suggest a lesser amount or suggest spreading the gift out over two to three years. Remind them of the charitable gift tax deduction.

If the plumber comes while you're meeting with them, or, if their daughter from across town drops in unexpectedly with her three-year old twins, graciously excuse yourself and agree to call for another appointment.

Should you take another person with you on the call? That's a judgment call. If your client is an older widow lady and you are a male, it might be preferable to take your wife with you or a woman friend of the client. If you know Ralph is a very good friend of theirs and would be influential with them, it might be wise to take him along. If you plan to do so, call ahead and ask if your prospects are comfortable with you bringing him along. If they resist, forget it. Except in extraordinary circumstances, never take more than one other person with you. If you take someone along, make it clear with him or her that you will do the talking; make the case. He/She is there for support.

The Call Back

Let's consider for a moment that you are not ready to make a formal proposal. Plans for the project are being considered by the appropriate group. The need is obvious. At this point you really just want to share the need with your prospect(s). You want to "share the dream" with them. Sometimes the strategy of sharing the dream privately with the client(s) can be a way of "testing the water" to get a reading on how they feel about the project, or to begin a process of involvement.

As mentioned before, Clarence Tompkins, a Methodist minister, now deceased, was assigned by the Iowa Conference to raise the funds to build a retirement facility in Fort Dodge, Iowa. Clarence started from scratch. He was a tireless worker. He devoted himself one hundred and fifty percent to raising the funds for the project. Several decades later, Friendship Haven, one of the finest retirement facilities in the Midwest, is serving hundreds of senior citizens.

Once when I called on Clarence — he was a graduate of Morningside College where I was working — he told me how he took a wealthy, elderly woman out on a tract of land owned by the retirement home, and shared with her his dream of a health center. The facility would have state-of-the art equipment, a highly-trained staff, and a program for elderly patients, including Alzheimer's victims, who needed special, loving care. Few people could describe such a dream with the passion and vision that wonderful man possessed. Later, the dear, generous woman made a huge lead gift and the health center became a reality.

The best strategy may be to share your dream with your client(s) and give God some time to work magic with them. Your dream may also become a reality.

Suppose for a moment, that you have done a good job of presenting your case. You did everything professionally. But, the prospect(s) declined to make the gift. There are many reasons why people decline to make a specific gift. Don't burn any bridges. Thank them graciously for considering the request. Making a major gift is a big decision. They may need some time to think about it, or to discuss it with others. They may feel sincerely bad that they aren't in a position to make the gift. No fundraiser hits a home run every time. Don't take a turn-down personally. Develop a plan and strategy for the next prospect. You can do it!

When the prospects have signed a pledge commitment be sure to write them a personal "thank you" note. And see that they receive at least two additional "thank you" notes from others. If they give consent, announce their commitment in your newsletter, omitting the amount of the gift. A word about the Statement of Intent: While I was doing professional fundraising, occasionally a prospect would indicate they planned to make a deferred gift. They needed time to talk with their family, their financial advisor, or their lawyer. That might take a few months.

In those cases, I would pull a copy of a Statement of Intent out of my briefcase and ask them to sign it. The Statement is not legally binding, but it gets the process started and can serve notice of the donor's honest intentions. A wise option is to provide the donor(s) a copy of the signed Statement of Intent to give to their attorney, or offer to send the copy to the attorney.

In one case while I was raising funds for the camping program, an older gentleman prospect told me he planned to give $100.000 either during his lifetime or in his will. He signed a Statement of Intent declaring his plan.

He died before informing his attorney or financial advisor. I presented a copy of the Statement of Intent to the Executor of his estate. The family contested the Statement. We went to court and the Judge decided in our favor. A check for $100,000 followed. If he had not signed the Statement of Intent the gift would have been lost.

There are copies of Statements of Intent for individuals and couples in the *Appendix*.

The Joy of Receiving the Check

Once in a while when I brought a large check home to the University, or to the Iowa Conference, in the case of the camps campaign, I felt for a moment like a Robin Hood. I had been successful in bringing some wealth to my institution where it would do a lot of good. Occasionally, when I would walk across the campus of the University and see the hundreds of students walking to class, I would wonder how many of them were there as the result of my work with donors. That is the joy of generating gifts for your cause, your church. You may be the key, and possibly the only key, to facilitating major gifts for your parish. You may not see the results during your ministry in this location. They may come a few years later in the form of a residence, a farm or an estate. But you will know that you were the key. You made it happen!

PROPOSAL GUIDE

Use the church's or denomination's letterhead.

May 5, 2010

To: Dr. and Mrs. Mark Weston
  322 Westown Parkway
  Anytown, USA

Dear Mary and Mark:

Introductory Paragraph (optional). "You are a very active member of Plymouth Church. You have served the church in many ways and have been and continue to be strong supporters of the church".

State Why You are Appealing To Them. Use your information on these prospects to establish a connection between them and the project which needs funding.

> "You will find this proposal of interest because it addresses a program in which you have been interested for several years."

> Or "You will be interested in this proposal because your dear mother, Mary Brown, was very interested in the (program or effort) for many years."

Needs Paragraph. Describe the need. Tailor the explanation to the thinking, values or interests of these donors.

> "You have been interested in the youth of our church for many years. You were leaders of the junior high and senior high programs when John and Ariel were in those groups.

> In the past 24 months thirty-five families have moved into the new development north of the church. There are 82 junior and senior high youth in those families. The potential for interesting those kids in the church is huge and very exciting.

Solution Paragraph. In three sentences or less describe your solution to the problem. How do you propose to solve the problem.

> "The Youth Council has decided that the church needs a full-time youth program director. That person would recruit and train adult leaders, develop programs for youth, and emphasize efforts to recruit additional youth."

Uniqueness Paragraph. Tell the prospective donors why your church or synagogue is the best choice for doing the job.

"Plymouth has an active program for children and junior highs. We need to do more with senior highs and especially with those in the new development."

"Plymouth Church is in a prime location to reach out to those kids."

Request For Funds. Describe how much the project will cost and how much money you are asking the donors to give.

"The salary, benefits, and office expenses for a full-time person is estimated to be $40,000, we are asking you to consider a leadership gift of $20,000 to fund half of the needed amount.

We plan to approach several other individuals and couples and ask them fund the other half."

Benefits to the Donors Paragraph. "Mary and David, by funding this youth leader position you will be making a huge contribution to the youth of the community and to the future of the church. Many of the youth will become active in the church as adults."

Closing Paragraph. "Thank you for considering the request. Please think about the proposal and pray about it. I will contact you in a few days to see what you have decided."

Double Heavyweight Signatures

Sincerely,   Sincerely,

Chair of the Youth Council   Chair of the Administration Board

Attachment: Detailed copy of the project budget

Chapter Ten

Building an Effective Fundraising Program

"Make no little plans; they have no magic to stir men's blood." DANIEL HUDSON BURNHAM

"But where no plan is laid, where the disposal of time is surrendered merely to the chance of incidents, all things lie huddled together in one chaos, which admits neither distribution nor review." HUGH BLAIR (1822)

Ameriprise, the financial management division of American Express, that was spun off three or four years ago, is currently running commercials. The central figure in the commercial repeats the mantra regarding retirement, "You need a plan. You can't start this journey without knowin' where you're goin'.'" And, in order to have an effective major gift program, you need a plan. The plan needs to be carefully thought through. It also needs to be written, with goals and objectives and a timeline or schedule. You will be much more successful, and will raise much more money if you build and execute a solid plan.

Keep in mind that a long-range plan for something as complex as a major gift program needs to be flexible. As circumstances change, as you become more skilled and effective, you may need to make mid-course corrections.

This book will have given you an overview of fundraising. In addition, if you can, plan to attend a seminar on fundraising designed for pastors and religious leaders. (See Chapter Eleven, *A Wide-Lens Perspective*, for agencies that offer such seminars and educational opportunities).

Your plan might include the following steps:

Step 1: To conceive and put in writing a three to five year plan for yourself. This plan is exclusively for you and not to be shared with anyone in your congregation. "This is what I hope to accomplish in this period of time." You also need to develop a three-to five-year plan for the finance committee and/or the deferred gift committee of your parish. Develop this plan in conjunction with your finance committee members. Obviously, the plans will be compatible but you want to keep your personal goals for the congregation separate and confidential.

Step 2: Your plan may include a three-month to six-month objective of educating yourself about money and financial matters in general and the economic environment of your community. Educating yourself is an on-going process, but the sooner you begin, the better. Go to the library and browse the *Investors Business Daily, Barron's, The Wall Street Journal, Money* or *Kiplinger's* magazines and the *Kiplinger Letter*. All are good sources of information on the economy, business and investments.

Step 3: You will need a confidential file in which to keep the information you glean on those members and constituents whom you have reason to believe have resources. Refer to the Prospect Information Form on Page 50.

Step 4: The plan for the Church may include the organization of a "Special Gifts Committee," "Deferred Gift" or "Second Mile Committee," whose role and function is to organize and conduct a program to encourage and facilitate deferred gifts to the Church. Estate planning attorneys, financial planners, professional fundraisers, tax advisors, certified public accountants, and bankers are good choices for this role. See the deferred gift material from the First Unitarian Church in Des Moines, located in the *Appendix*.

Step 5: An important feature in your plan is a communication plan that sets out objectives for providing the congregation information about deferred gifts, tax advantages, making a will, and related subjects. Informing the congregation of the possible opportunities for major and deferred gifts will help to encourage people to consider those possibilities. The "Special Gifts Committee" may assume this responsibility, but, as pastor, you need to see that the job gets done.

Step 6: If you are a pastor of a large congregation, say, a thousand or more members, you may want to think about employing a full or part-time person to also do major and deferred gift work for the church.

I know of one United Church of Christ which, when seeking to hire a financial manager for the congregation, chose a person who had some fundraising experience. A retired attorney, CPA, or financial advisor might be a prime candidate for a part-time position. Or, that person might be willing to do some of this work on a volunteer basis. Regardless, whether or not you have such a person does not relieve you of the responsibility of being personally involved in the fundraising process.

Step 7: Begin the process of gathering and recording information on your prospective members. See Chapter Five, "The Millionaire in the Pew" on gathering information. Also, refer to the graphic on Page 14 that outlines the fundraising process.

Step 8: Organize a "Heritage Circle" or "Future Society" or "The Bequeather's Society" for people who have included a bequest in their will to the Church. Persuade a few people to lead the way and announce their decision to the congregation. Encourage others to join this group. (Please see the Heritage Circle enrollment form at the end of this chapter.)

Step 9: Plan for a series of seminars on estate planning, family financial planning, deferred gifting, and related subjects. You can usually find competent people in your community who are willing to lead seminars on these subjects. The universities, colleges, and community colleges have trained people who would probably provide this leadership as a contribution. If your denomination has a foundation, the director of the foundation will be happy to provide that service.

Step 10: Establish a relationship with, and provide literature to the attorneys in your community. Visit with them about supporting your major and deferred gift program. Provide them with the legal name of your congregation and urge them to encourage potential donors to remember "Old First Church" in their estate plan. Better yet, invite them to a free lunch at which you provide that information.

Step 11: Related to your research on individuals or families, keep your eyes and ears open to the existence of family and community trusts. Those may be a great source of funds. Information on trusts is usually public information.

Step 12: A study conducted by the Center on Philanthropy at Indiana University shows that high-net-worth donors rely on fundraisers and personnel from non-profit organizations for information on giving more than on their own financial advisors or lawyers. Knowledgeable pastors can serve that purpose and make people aware of the needs of the Church.

The foundation of an effective stewardship and major gift program is a communication program that keeps the congregation informed about what the Church is doing. Today's church members are more interested in performance, in what is being done, accomplished. Lyle Schaller puts it this way:

> "In the old ecclesiastical economy, credibility often was institution-based. In the new ecclesiastical economy, credibility is increasingly performance-based. This is especially true for the generations born after World War II. Younger Americans are far more likely than older ones to challenge the credibility of corporations, governmental agencies, political parties, hospitals, military officers, physicians, denominational officials, professors, civil servants, the news media, and experts in general.
> For most congregations, this means improving the system of internal communication to help people understand more fully all aspects of the ministry. The guiding generalization is the larger the size of the congregation, the larger the proportion of the constituents who are unaware of most of what is happening."[1]

Building and working your plan will require effort. It may involve doing some new and different thinking on your part. But, believe me, it will pay off. It will bring results. A final comment — building a successful program, especially for deferred gifts, may take several years. If you are starting from scratch, it may be several years before you see any results. Also, keep in mind that some people put an organization in their will and do not inform the recipient. You may not see any deferred gift results while serving this congregation. But your successors will. Plant the seeds and the harvest will come. You can do it. A word of advice:

Don't attempt to assume leadership for a capital campaign in your own parish. Or, for that matter, in another parish. Leading a successful capital campaign requires a major investment of time and effort. It is a full-time job. You already have a full-time job. You cannot possibly take on another. Hire a professional.

---

1   Schaller, Lyle E., *The New Context For Ministry*, Abingdon Press, Nashville, TN, 2002, 163

THE HERITAGE CIRCLE

The Heritage Circle of St. Mark's Church at Maple Street and Benton Avenue, in Kansas City, Missouri, is dedicated to the future ministry and mission of St. Mark's church. The members of the Heritage Circle undergird the future of the church by providing a bequest in their Wills.

The commitment of the members of the Heritage Circle will help to continue the work of the church far into the future.

_____I, _____We, wish to become members of the Heritage Circle.

_____I, _____We, have made provision for a bequest to St. Mark's Church in our will(s).

The bequest is in the form of_____cash, or a_____percentage of_____my,_____our, estate, or,

(other)_____

The bequest may be used where the need is greatest_____, or as follows: _____

_____

A copy of the will is located in the office of my/our attorney:_____

_____A copy of the page of the will referring to the bequeath is attached.

The presence of your name(s) will encourage others to include St. Mark's in their wills. The church would like to add your name(s) to the list of members of the Heritage Circle.

_____I, _____We give consent to have our name(s) listed among the members of the Heritage Circle, and available to the members of the church.

_____I, _____We choose to have the bequest kept confidential

_____I, _____We would like the bequest identified in memory of (please print):

_____

_____I, _____We, choose not to identify a memorial.

Signed _____ Date _____

Address _____

Signed _____ Date_____

Address_____

Chapter Eleven

A Wide Lens Perspective

Your efforts to build and maintain a solid and effective major and deferred gift program are not conducted in a vacuum. You will have to work within the economic environment of your congregation and your community.

Many factors will come into play as you plan and execute your program. You will need to consider the general financial condition of your town or community. How robust or weak is the economy? Are your people feeling optimistic or pessimistic about their jobs, the economy, and their financial futures?

Another factor is the ages of your members. A young suburban congregation will not have the potential for major and deferred gifts that a long-established congregation will have. The giving history of the congregation is important. How well have they supported the Church and its programs in the past?

On September 11, 2001, I was having breakfast in the McDonald's in Clear Lake, Iowa. An acquaintance informed me of the attack on the World Trade Center in New York City. I was conducting a campaign to raise funds for the camps in the Iowa Conference of the United Methodist Church and had appointments to call on people in the area that day. I cancelled the appointments and headed home.

That event changed the attitudes of people toward giving for over a year. People were apprehensive. The future was unknown. People became more conservative. It was much more difficult to raise funds. We even considered the possibility of putting the campaign on hold until the pessimism and fear subsided. This is an extreme example of how circumstances can influence the environment in which fund raising is being done. Obviously, since the country is currently in a recession (2011), this may not be the best time to ask for current major gifts. The economy will eventually recover and the environment for fundraising will improve.

In 1964, I was appointed by the then Governor, Harold E. Hughes, to the Board of Control of State Institutions of the State of Iowa. The board was a full-time board responsible for the policy and administration of thirteen state institutions. Included were the prisons, mental hospitals, hospital schools for special needs people, two homes for homeless and neglected children, a reform school, and a home for veterans.

In order to keep one foot in the Church I accepted a part-time appointment to a small church in State Center, Iowa. I could be in the office in Des Moines during the week and serve the relatively-small congregation on weekends. After the service on the second or third Sunday there, on a beautiful warm spring day, several of the men gathered in a circle out on the lawn. They beckoned me to join them and in so many words said, "This old church is about to fall down. We think you can provide the leadership to help us build a new church." What a challenge! We razed the old building and built a new sanctuary. And paid for it. The time was ripe. The economic environment was favorable. The majority of the members were farmers and they were doing well. The climate was right and those men knew it.

Stewardship Education for the Future

Another and extremely important factor that affects the long range potential for gifts is the money management or lack of money management of your congregants. This is especially important if your congregation is in the 30–50 age range. If people do not manage their money well, or if they are caught up in the "spend yourself out of debt" epidemic that has spread throughout our society they cannot possibly make major contributions to the Church.

Fortunately, some churches are taking constructive action and are providing seminars on budgeting and money management. Connie Gilmore, a good friend of my wife and me, who lives in Las Vegas, has recently led seminars for people in debt called Financial Peace University.

That program is available through the Dave Ramsey organization (www.daveramsey.com). Included in the seminar are great videos by Dave Ramsey that are the focal point of each of the 10–12 two-hour sessions. A leader's guide and participant's workbooks flesh out the sessions. Ramsey is a superb presenter. He is bright and very well informed. His sense of humor is delightful. Financial Peace University helps people manage their finances and get out of debt. Ramsey understands the Church and encourages generosity.

In a recent session of Financial Peace University, Connie had seven families enrolled. They anonymously submitted their household debt, not including their mortgage. Their total was an astounding $504,000! The highest was $183,000, the lowest was $4,900.

As a result of the sessions led by Connie, many couples and individuals have gotten out of debt and have gained control of their finances. I highly recommend the sessions. A financial professional — a banker, financial advisor, insurance executive, business or economics teacher or faculty member or fundraiser — could lead the seminars.

Another source of financial education for Christians, about which I know very little, but which has an excellent reputation is Crown Financial Ministries. Organized by Larry Burkett, now deceased, Crown Financial Ministers was originally known as Christian Financial Concepts. *Website Address:* www.crown.org

The book, *Money and the Meaning of Life*, by Jacob Needleman, would be a great book for a church study group. It includes questions for discussion. I highly recommend it.

Another great resource for individuals or groups to read and discuss is the book,

Give to Live, How Giving Can Change Your Life, by Douglas M. Lawson. In fact, Lawson offers a variety of materials on stewardship and giving. He also offers, *A Complete Stewardship Program For Your Church*, available through Abingdon Press. Consult your local religious bookstore for more information.

An excellent resource for educators on the topic of fund raising and philanthropy is the Center on Philanthropy at Indiana University. They offer several seminars on development including one on Faith and Fundraising. Contact them and ask them to put you on their mailing list to receive their reports. *Web Address:* www.philanthropy.iupui.edu

The National Development Institute in Columbia, South Carolina, is another excellent resource for religious leaders. They offer seminars on "Faith and Fundraising." They do an excellent job. Their presentations would apply to pastors, priests, rabbis, and denominational leaders, as well as to lay leaders. *Phone Number:* 803.808.0537. *Web Address:* www.nationaldevelopmentinstitute.org

The Stewardship Academy sponsored by the Bishop Ruben Job Center for Learning Development, in Indiana, offers excellent seminars on stewardship for pastors and religious leaders. The Rev. Dr. Wayne Barrett, President and Executive Director of the United Methodist Foundation of the Michigan Conference, is a leader of the Stewardship Academy and has many years of experience in stewardship and fundraising. He has written many papers and books on the subject and is a wonderful resource. Dr. Barrett can be reached at the United Methodist Foundation of Michigan. *Phone Number:* 1.800.451.1929. *Web Address:* www.UMFMichigan.org

The Ecumenical Stewardship Center, 5300 Annapolis Lane North #4330, Plymouth, MN, 55446. This is a wonderful source of conferences, education, networking and materials about — you guessed it — stewardship. *Phone Number:* 855.278.4372 (4ESC). *Email Address:* office@stewardshipresources.org

Another great source of stewardship and fundraising education is the Lake Institute on Faith and Giving, located on the campus of Indiana University. The Institute is closely related to the Center on Philanthropy mentioned before. They offer a variety of educational opportunities for clergy and congregations. One is entitled, "Creating Congregational Cultures of Generosity." *Web Address:* www.philanthropy.iupui.edu/LakeFamilyInstitute

Many denominations provide resources for education in financial planning. For example, The Board of Discipleship of the United Methodist Church has a study guide, *Christians Doing Financial Planning*. The Center for Parish Development in Chicago also has excellent materials on stewardship. *Web Address:* www.missionalchurch.org

My good friend and former mentor, Dr. Paul Dietterich, was for many years the Executive Director of the Center for Parish Development. Paul was the resource person, teacher and consultant for a five-year project conducted in the Waterloo District of the United Methodist Church in Iowa. The experiment, entitled, *An Experiment in District Revitalization,* was the brain child of the then District Superintendent, Rev. Don Arthur, now deceased. The experiment was an attempt to apply the principles of leadership, organizational development, communication, team building, goal setting and other "management" disciplines to breathe new life and vitality into the Waterloo area that included some 60 United Methodist Churches.

For five years, Paul came to Waterloo and spent one day per month with Don and me, and a second day with us and the members of the District Council on Ministries. In addition to doing training with the members of the District Council and with clusters of local pastors, I was assigned to apply the learnings shared by Paul, to a local church, Shell Rock, and to mentor the young pastor, Rev. Jim Dotson. Paul and I co-authored a report on the work that I did with the Shell Rock congregation entitled, *A Process of Local Church Vitalization*.[1] It is available from the Center for Parish Development.

Among the spin-offs of that extensive five-year effort was a definitive work on stewardship entitled, *A System Approach to Stewardship*.[2] Although copyrighted in 1976, it is as timeless as the U.S. Constitution. If it, or a revision, is still available, I highly recommend it.

Paul and his wife, Inagrace Dietterich, have authored several outstanding works on stewardship and financial development. One is entitled, *Stewards of the Household of God*, by Inagrace. The companion publication, *Pastor's Resource Booklet,* is a must for your library. Another publication, *Stewards of God's Gifts, A Resource for Studying the Biblical Understanding of Stewardship*, by Paul and Inagrace, is a rich resource. Paul, and a colleague, Carl Diederichs, a professional fundraiser, wrote *Developing Financial Stewardship, A Resource for Cultivating Christian Stewardship for use with Church Leaders.* These are all excellent resources.

These and many other top-drawer, highly-professional resources are available from The Center for Parish Development, 1525 E. 55th Street Suite 201, Chicago, IL, 60615. *Phone Number:* 1.773.752.1596. *Fax Number:* 1.773.752.5093.

A great source of guidance on setting up an endowment and planned giving program in a local church is the Moravian Ministry Foundation in America. They provide policies and procedures. *Phone Number (toll-free):* 1.888.722.7923. *Email Address:* paul@mmfa.info

Elsewhere in this book we have discussed the hazards of this materialistic culture. We have highlighted the crippling effects of over spending, overextending one's self or family. Family financial seminars and workshops accomplish two important objectives.

One, they teach people to live within their means and two, they help people get into a position that they can contribute financially to the Church and community.

Financial planning education will also help your people to save for the future. People who spend every dime they get are setting themselves up for a poverty-level retirement — how tragic. The church can help its people to manage and to save for the future.

Don't expect instant results. Some of these spending, wasting, over consuming, "spend yourself out of debt" habits and practices are deeply ingrained. Remember, however, "inch by inch, anything's a cinch." We're talking about a long process. But it has to begin somewhere. You can do it!

---

1   Dietterich, Paul and Wilson, Russell, *A Process of Local Church Vitalization,* The Center for Parish Development, Chicago, IL, 1976

2   *A System Approach to Stewardship,* Center for Parish Development, Chicago, IL, 1976

Chapter Twelve

A Bald Eagle Feather and a Village in India — Generosity

"This spirit (within us) manifests itself in many ways, but virtually all spirituality is grounded in two vital principles: the need to do good for one another and the need to love and respect one another." DR. DOUGLAS M. LAWSON

"Giving and sharing not only help others, they also give us life." DR. DOUGLAS M. LAWSON

A grandfather is speaking,

> "It is almost midnight. In a few hours I will enter the hospital for major heart surgery, a triple bypass. This evening I had supper with one of my sons and his family. My five-year-old grandson, Ian, presented me with an envelope and his best wishes. Inside the envelope was a single feather.
>
> His mother explained, 'Ian has a box in his room; he calls it his treasure chest. He keeps all of his favorite things in it. This is a feather from a bald eagle; it was given to him at a gathering of first-nations people several months ago. It has been his favorite treasure ever since.' Suddenly the feather took on a whole new meaning for me; it was no longer just a pretty and unusual gift. My grandson had given me his most precious possession because he loves me. It reminded me of the poor widow whom Jesus praised for putting all she had into the treasury."[1]

In 1995, just before Christmas, Malden Mills, a textile mill in Lawrence, Massachusetts, burned to the ground. Owner, Aaron Feuerstein, made the decision to rebuild on the same spot, resisting the temptation to move south where cheaper labor would have been available. Out of his own pocket, Feuerstein extended the salaries of the 3,000 employees of the mill for another month. In his booklet, *Can Generosity Be Taught?*, Laurence Daloz writes, "His (Feuerstein's) actions garnered considerable press, and he was hailed as an altruist. But Feuerstein, raised in a traditional Jewish home with a history of civic involvement, does not see it that way at all. When he told a reporter, 'I don't deserve credit,' he was not being disingenuous. 'Corporate America,' he went on, 'has made it so that when you behave the way I did, it's abnormal.'"[2]

Feuerstein implies that it is the system that is defective, and that his behavior was that of a "normal, respectable" human being. "A certain generosity," he seems to be saying, "is normal. It is greed that is not."[3]

Feuerstein was acting out of recognition that, as human beings, we have a responsibility to one another. We are part of the larger society and share responsibility for the total. "'I have a responsibility to the worker… [but] I have an equal responsibility to the community,' Feuerstein is reported as saying."[4]

On October 14, 1976, Vicki Dischner gave birth to a baby girl, Tasha, a premature baby. Tasha lived only two months. Grief-stricken, Vicki could not find the baby a little dress or a tiny casket. Vicki's grandmother made a little dress using a doll pattern. A makeshift casket was made from cardboard.

Vicki was so impressed with the need for tiny burial clothing and caskets that she began making those items and giving them to indigent couples who had lost a baby. Thirty-one years later Vicki is still making baby burial clothing and caskets and giving them to parents who can't afford them. She recruits volunteers to sew burial outfits for boys and girls, casket linings, pillows, blankets and tiny teddy bears. She also recruits volunteer woodworkers to make little caskets. She ships an average of 240 sets per year to indigent couples in hospitals all over the United States.

Vicki is not a wealthy woman. For years she has worked as a nurse's aid and contributed about $10,000 annually to support the program. Yes, $10,000 per year! — on a minimal salary, plus hours and hours devoted to making and lining little caskets, recruiting volunteers, securing contributions of lumber and fabric, and shipping items. Vicki is a selfless, compassionate and generous woman.

In December of 1988, a young Ph.D. student at the University of Minnesota flew to Bombay, India. She had chosen, as her Ph.D. research thesis project, to go to a typical village in India and do hands-on, experimental research on *What Can Be Done to Help Women in a Typical Village Help Themselves?*

She settled and lived for a year in a remote village of 1,500. Poverty and illiteracy were the norm. She helped to organized the women, 120 of them, into the "Women's Circle." Only one woman out of the 120 could read and write. After preparing supper and putting the children to bed, the women would meet to discuss their dreams of improving life in the village. Their first priority was to provide a high school for the girls. The closest high school was five miles away, an impossible walk for boys or girls during the monsoon. No girls and few boys made the effort.

The graduate student appealed to her family and friends and they raised enough funds to build two classrooms and to hire a teacher. Twenty-six girls attended the first class. The school became so popular that it was soon opened to boys. In 1995, when June, my wife, and I visited the village, there were 96 boys and girls in the school — so many that they had to have a morning and an afternoon session.

Today, several hundred students have graduated from the school and many have gone on to college. One has graduated from medical school.

The Ph.D. graduate student is our daughter, Dr. Clarice Auluck-Wilson, who lives in Stillwater, Minnesota, with her family. At great sacrifice she gave a year of her life and personally contributed considerable financial resources for the women and children in the village and is still causing thousands of dollars to be contributed to the school and to the post-high education of the students.

It is easy to identify the generosity of Bill and Melinda Gates who have given millions to deserving causes. It is not so easy to identify the thousands of people in our neighborhoods, towns and cities who commit acts of generosity every day. I refer to those who have chosen service careers in which the salaries are modest, including teachers, counselors, social workers, clergy, nurses, nurses' aides, and many others. Their professions include staff members of homeless shelters, community service centers, Goodwill Industries, and many other non-profit agencies. Many of those people are making generous contributions every day to the people they serve. Because of their generosity, the community is blessed.

Although in this book we are thinking primarily of generosity with money, many people are generous with time, knowledge, energy, and influence. If, for instance, a congregation would take a survey of the contributions their members make in volunteer service, the number of hours served would be impressive. Volunteers serve homeless shelters, food banks, and hospitals. They serve as tutors, teachers of English as a second language, classroom assistants, and in many other ways.

There is no relationship between the value of the gift or gifts and the quality of generosity. Jesus demonstrated that fact when he honored the widow who gave her penny. Generosity, motivated by self-sacrifice and desire to help others, is noble and honorable regardless of the value of the gift. "He who gives all, though but little, gives much: because God looks not to the quality of the gift, but to the quality of the giver," quoted the English author, Francis Quarles.[5]

As you may know, I spent many years doing fund raising for churches, a private church-related college, and a major state university. During those years I raised millions of dollars for those institutions. I had opportunities to work with many very wonderful and generous people. I saw churches built, research programs funded, scholarship funds created, and academic chairs endowed. I also saw new buildings built and others refurbished, technologies installed, rural extension programs supported, and many other wonderful things happen — all, the result of the generosity of people.

Actually, every day of our lives you and I are the benefactors of the generosity of others. When we attended college, university and seminary we were the recipients of the generosity of others. They built buildings, funded academic chairs, and supported faculty. When you and I visit the local library, the hospital, the zoo, the art center, the YMCA or YWCA, the science center, the aquarium, the theatre, or listen to public radio or television, we are enjoying the results of the generosity of others.

I recently sat with my cousin, Jo Childs, whose husband Dr. Carroll Childs, was dying in a local hospice. On the wall in the foyer is a donor recognition "tree," the brass leaves of which are inscribed with the names of those whose contributions helped to build the facility. My cousin, her husband, our family, and many other families are the benefactors of their generosity.

If you were born in a hospital, the hospital was no doubt funded in part by contributions. If you die in a hospice, you and your family will be the benefactors of the generosity of others. From birth to death and every day of our lives we benefit from other's generosity. Thousands of students, who have been economically, socially or psychologically disadvantaged because of family circumstances, will be able to attend Iowa State University. Why? — Because of Christina Hixson, a philanthropist in Las Vegas. Ms. Hixson gave millions to establish a scholarship fund for such students.

An eagle feather given by a five-year-old, a widow's penny, a manufacturer's Christmas paychecks, a woman providing little baby caskets, a young woman providing a high school for girls in a village in India, and a woman funding scholarships for thousands of disadvantaged students — all motivated by generosity.

Generosity ranks among the highest, most noble-minded, most magnanimous, and spiritual of all human qualities. For me, it ranks along with love, faith and the Golden Rule.

If you consult your dictionary or thesaurus for the meaning of "generosity", you will find such descriptions as magnanimous, gracious, great-hearted, unselfish, high-principled, having qualities associated with noble birth, queen-like, noble, chivalrous, willing to share, and altruistic. Dr. Lawson describes generous people as "spiritual to the core of their being."

These words and phrases describe the highest, most spiritually developed, most giving, and most high-principled people on earth. The cream of the cream.

Many generous people possess the quality of empathy; they can emotionally and psychologically walk in another's shoes. They are able to identify with another's pain, suffering, anguish or loss. Most generous people are able to make a distinction between their true needs, their "wants" and "the must-haves" that the materialistic, commercial world tells them they need.

Generous people are willing to share what they have, whether they possess modest means or billions, with those in need.

As demonstrated by Aaron Feuerstein, the manufacturer who rebuilt his destroyed plant in the same community, because he felt a responsibility to that community, many generous people have a sense of responsibility to their community. Their sense of community may extend to the other side of the globe.

Generous people often enjoy a sense of satisfaction that by joining with others, by pooling their resources, so to speak, they are able to accomplish great things that they could never have accomplished alone. Generous people enjoy many physical and emotional and spiritual benefits as we will discuss later in this chapter.

I have included this discussion about generosity, and included these moving stories of generosity for several reasons. In the first place, I think that we should give the concept of generosity, the concept of selfless giving, the place of value and high honor that it deserves. We need to honor acts of generosity and recognize the tremendous good that is accomplished by generous people.

Secondly, I believe that by emphasizing generosity and lifting up the qualities of generous people in the minds of our parishioners, we transform giving from an obligation, a burden, to a source of joy, of satisfaction and fulfillment.

The third reason for emphasizing generosity is that I believe an appeal to generosity is a far more effective and compelling motivator for giving to the Church and community than most traditional approaches. Tithing, as a concept, is held up by many clergy as the biblical standard of giving to the Church. Some include giving to church and the community in the tithe. However, tithing is a rigid and legalistic concept that places a much heavier burden on low income people than on the wealthy. A regressive tax, if you please. The tithe sets the bar of responsibility much lower for the wealthy, whom it may be argued, have greater resources and thus, have greater responsibility for giving. It is hard for me to make a case for tithing in the New Testament. If, by promoting tithing as the goal and obligation, your people are motivated to provide amply for your ministry and mission, power to you and to them. However, please consider also lifting up the concept of generosity. Your people will enjoy giving their tithes more and feel better as a result.

Proportionate giving, another approach to the practice of stewardship is a practical approach to giving, but it seems to me to lack the motivation, the appeal to the emotions, the sense of spiritual commitment inherent in the teachings of Jesus and the Apostle Paul.

An appeal to generosity

— *based on* a sense of gratitude for all that God has given to me…

— *based on* the recognition that all that I have and all that I am is a gift of God…

— *based on* an honorable sense of responsibility to my fellow man…

— *based on* the awareness that by pooling my gifts with others in the Church, regardless how great or small they are, I am able to do great things to change the world…

— *based on* the awareness that I am joining a great company of noble and generous people…

is, for me a far more exciting and more compelling appeal to giving, a far more powerful motivator.

An appeal to generosity is an appeal to one's most magnanimous self, one's highest character, one's most honorable and charitable motives. Generous people are wonderful people. The world is a much more wonderful and hospitable place because of them and their gifts.

It seems to me that to appeal to people's highest nature, to appeal to the compelling and spiritual quality of generosity, as exemplified by thousands of unselfish and caring people, is more powerful. It speaks to one's need and one's desire to contribute, to give, to become a member of that association of giving people, those altruistic and magnanimous members of the Church.

Generosity is a response to several motivating factors. We dealt with those factors or motivators in Chapter Seven. You may want to review that chapter in regard to the issue of what motivates people to be generous.

The Physical, Psychological, and Spiritual Benefits of Altruism

Rev. Dr. Douglas M. Lawson is an ordained minister who is also a highly successful professional fundraiser. His books, *Give to Live* and *More Give to Live*, are classics. In them he discusses, with passion and spiritual sensitivity, the many physical, psychological, and spiritual benefits of giving, of altruism. With his personal permission, I have quoted his books extensively because they are a rich source of his experience and research on the subject. I found the material both enlightening and inspiring. I hope you will find it so, as well. Dr. Lawson says that "Giving and sharing not only help others, they also give us life."[6] It is obvious that generosity benefits the recipients. It is not so obvious that generous people also receive rich benefits. "They live longer and live happier."[2]

> "Professor Mihaly Csikszentmihalyi, of the University of Chicago has for many years conducted a detailed inquiry into the psychology of peak experiences. In his acclaimed work *Flow: The Psychology of Peak Experience*, he examines emotional factors necessary for people to experience the pleasurable, health-sustaining, mental state he describes as 'flow.' His findings prove the benefits of philanthropic behavior.
> "These new studies tell us that assisting others, through acts of charity or devotion to causes, improves our physical well-being. Giving is not just a minor influence on good health but the key to bodily and mental well-being. The studies show that for all ages (but particularly among the elderly), one way to escape premature physical and emotional deterioration is by staying active in the service of others."[7]

"A ten-year study of 2,700 men in Tecumseh, Michigan, found that the men who were active in volunteer work had death rates two and one-half times lower than men who did not."[8]

Dr. Norman Vincent Peale quoted a study conducted by a life insurance company, of policy holders who were one hundred years or older. When asked what was the most important thing they had learned, the answer most often given was, 'to love thy neighbor as thyself.' Dr. Peale concludes: "They live longer... because they have freed themselves from deadly negative influences such as anger, hatred, suspicion, guilt, and anxiety. These toxic emotions can lead to cynicism, hostility and isolation, traits that Dr. Dean Ornish, noted heart specialist, identifies as major components of heart disease, high blood pressure, stroke, and probably cancer."[9]

Dr. Herbert Benson, a heart specialist, was quoted in Psychology Today, in regard to the benefits of giving: "For millennia, people have been describing techniques on how to forget oneself, how to experience decreased metabolic rates, lower blood pressure, lower heart rates and other health benefits. Altruism works this way, just as do yoga, spirituality and meditation."[10]

Dr. Hans Selye, who is known as the "father of stress reduction" spent years studying the relationship between stress and illness. Selye coined the phrase, "altruistic ego" to describe people who are involved in philanthropic activities. Selye quotes, " ' The love and gratitude we inspire in those we help...is a valuable payback." He wrote, "like stress, love has a cumulative effect.'"[11] Commenting on Selye's statements, Lawson says, "This captures the essence of this book [Lawson's]: sustained good deeds have a cumulative positive effect on our well-being."[12]

"In a pioneering investigation of 1,500 women volunteers, by sociologist Allen Luks, many subjects mentioned the enjoyable physical sensations they experienced while helping others and for some time afterward. Luks concluded that this 'helper's high' reduces the emotional stress that interferes with the body's self-maintenance system. He went on to say, 'These stresses cause the adrenal glands to release stress chemicals… that increase cholesterol levels that play a role in heart disease, raise blood sugar, and depress the immune system.' In contrast, the women Luks investigated spoke of increased energy, a satisfying state of calm, and a feeling of warmth and well-being,"[13] quotes Lawson.

"These emerging findings of the powerful benefits of philanthropic activity point chiefly to volunteers and face-to-face involvement. But there is a link with financial donations as well. When people give significant amounts of money, personal involvement usually follows since interest, concern and commitment accompany most gifts of money. Instead of the old slogan 'Give until it hurts,' it seems we should say, 'Give until you feel great,'" quotes Lawson.[14]

We have discussed the physical benefits of helping others and exercising generosity. Now, let's look at the research on the psychological benefits of giving. It is not easy to achieve and maintain a sense of emotional equilibrium, especially today. Life is full of conflicts, disappointments, and challenges. Financial problems, marital and family conflicts, loneliness and boredom erode many people's sense of well being, of inner peace and contentment.

"But," Dr. Lawson reports,

"… there is one kind of experience that delivers emotional and psychic satisfaction time after time, day after day: helping other people. Volunteer efforts, charitable acts, generosity of spirit, and gestures of compassion all enrich and sustain our lives….

Volunteering our resources and talents without thought of gain showers benefits on us we may never have expected…. A stronger, better defined sense of self emerges through giving. Inner approval, feeling more positive about oneself — these are emotional benefits volunteers and donors cite in describing their feelings about acts of generosity."[15]

"Volunteering and giving enhance self-acceptance. Emotional transference takes place during volunteer activity. In giving love and concern to others we receive love, gratitude, and acceptance in return. The recently published book *Healthy Pleasures* puts it this way: 'We can get a special kind of attention from those we help. This sincere gratitude can be very [emotionally] nourishing. Like the impoverishment of sensuality, we lack healthy doses of genuine appreciation and heartfelt thanks for our good actions. Most of us need such thanks from others, and need to feel that we matter to someone.' It follows that the more we help others, the more we gain in self-appreciation and emotional well-being,"[16] quotes Lawson.

In *The Broken Heart — The Medical Consequences of Loneliness*, Dr. James Lynch of the University of Maryland School of Medicine says,

"'Love your neighbor as you love yourself' is not just a moral mandate. It's a physiological mandate. Caring is biological. One thing you get from caring is that you are not lonely, and the more connected you are to life, the healthier you are.' Community and connectedness have long been acknowledged as important influences on mental health by the medical and psychiatric professions."[17]

In *More Give to Live*, this statement affirms the value of giving:

"Dr. Dean Ornish, in *A Program for Reversing Heart Disease*, cites self-centeredness, the habitual use of the pronoun "*I*," and emotional isolation as destructive to emotional and physical health. People need good relationships with other people their whole life long. Newborn infants do not survive if they are not loved and nurtured, nor do the elderly. And even during our middle years, when we are most self-reliant, we are vulnerable. Giving and sharing not only help others, they also give us life."[18]

Generosity, giving, and helping others also contribute to one's spiritual health and growth. Lawson writes,

"*Acts to help others have positive effects on our spiritual well-being*. Hundreds of people over the years have shared with me the benefits they've derived from giving. In humble and eloquent detail they have described moments of joy, peace of mind, satisfaction, and inner acceptance. When people give to their fellow man, something special happens. They are blessed with an extra dimension of inner harmony.

Philanthropy is a way of life for some people, dedicated benefactors who are spiritual to the core of their being."[19]

He continues,

"When people tell me philanthropy has changed their lives, opened up new vistas, brought renewed compassion and love to their spirit, I believe what they say is true. However inarticulate a person's description may be, good deeds enlarge the heart and strengthen the soul. Spirituality and religion are forces that preserve the best in mankind. People aren't born with an abiding faith or peace of mind. They develop it in doing good deeds for others, acting to put their beliefs into practice.

A good deed, what the Torah calls *mitzvah*, connects us to the goodness of God, increases the righteousness in the world, decreases the alienation and evil, helps our neighbor, enhances our self-appreciation, and makes everyone — ourselves included — richer."[20]

1   This material is reprinted from *The Upper Room Magazine,* copyright 2007, by the Upper Room, Inc., P.O. Box 340004, Nashville, TN 37203-0004, October 22, 2007, and with permission of Lloyd Kitching, the author.

2   Daloz, Laurent A., *Can Generosity Be Taught?,* published by the Center on Philanthropy of Indiana University, Indianapolis, IN, 1998, 1

3   *Parade Magazine,* September 8, 1996, 5, quoted in Daloz, Laurent A., *Can Generosity Be Taught?,* published by the Center on Philanthropy, Indiana University, Indianapolis, IN, 1998

4   Ibid.

5   Edwards, Tyron, D.D., *New Dictionary of Thoughts,* Family Library Club, Cincinnati, OH, 1950

6   Lawson, Douglas M., *Give to Live,* ALTI Publishing, LaJolla, CA, 1991, 28

7   Ibid.

8   Ibid., 24

9   Ibid., 20

10   Ibid.

11   Ibid., 32–33

12   Ibid., 33

13   Ibid., 23

14   Lawson, Douglas M., *More Give to Live,* ALTI Publishing, LaJolla, CA, 1991, 22

15   Ibid., 23

16   Ibid.

17   Ibid., 24–25

18   Ibid.

19   Ibid., 26

20   Ibid., 27

ACKNOWLEDGEMENTS

I am grateful for the encouragement and support of my friend, David Ruhe, who, from the beginning, recognized the potential value of *The Millionaire in the Pew.* Another individual to whom I am grateful is Stephen Gray, who not only encouraged me but also guided me to some rich resources, including the creative work that the United Church of Christ is doing.

Rich Pleva provided advice and read portions of the manuscript which was very helpful. The staff of the Center on Philanthropy at Indiana University provided valuable articles and reports of research that were current and scientifically grounded, that added a valuable dimension of academic credibility to the book. The encouragement and support of Bishop Julius Trimble and his assistant, Bob Burkhart, were very helpful.

Bob Coffman was helpful in editing the manuscript and giving professional advice on a number of important aspects of the book.

Nicki Wynn provided word processing in the beginning and Michelle Riesenberg came to my rescue with her trusty computer and her patience when word processing and numerous revisions and changes were necessary. They were very helpful.

I am indebted to the following authors as their work provided valuable information on important subjects which I felt were important but about which my knowledge was quite limited. They include: Lyle Schaller, Patrick Rooney, Paul and Inagrace Dietterich, Douglas M. Lawson, William Danko, Thomas Stanley, Dwight Burlingame, and Kevin Hogan. Their works are quoted throughout the book.

And to our daughter, Connie, and granddaughter, Avalan, both graphic designers, for their hours of design, formatting and organization of the book. I'm not sure the book would ever have been completed without their untiring help.

And of course, my wife June, my partner for over 60 years, who read the manuscript, made suggestions, and provided valuable feedback on a number of issues.

My thanks and gratitude to all.

Russ Wilson

The following is a document that was distributed in the First Unitarian Church of Des Moines, Iowa, that focused on establishing endowment funds for the Church. It is copied for your reference and meant to serve as a model as you create your own document.

First Unitarian Endowment Fund Recognition Weekend[1]

It is with great pleasure that the Endowment Fund Committee of First Unitarian Church recognizes members of the newly established Legacy Society and Chalice Society.

Legacy Society

Members of the Legacy Society have indicated that they have made arrangements in their estate plans for funds to come to the Endowment Fund. *Members of the Legacy Society include:*

Jane Bell
Tom Bierly
Steve and Karen Herwig
David Proudfit
Barb Royal
Deidre Fudge
Dwight and Beth Sanders
Barry Ulberg

Chalice Society

Members of the Chalice Society have made contributions of one thousand dollars or more either as accumulated gifts or a one-time gift. *Members of the Chalice Society include:*

Jane Bell
Ann Mowery and Al Powers
Charlotte Shivvers

Many members have in the past made known that their estate plans include the Endowment Fund or have made significant contributions to the Fund. You may find their names on plaques in the church's entry hall.

In its growth, the Endowment Fund plays an important role in ensuring the long term financial stability of First Unitarian Church of Des Moines. It has also become a vibrant part of the programming at First Unitarian with the use of a portion of the interest from the Fund's investments for the provision of Radical Engagement and Creative Happenings (REACH) grants. The purpose of REACH grants is to provide funds, beyond usual budget constraints, for projects which REACH out into the larger community or deepen and widen our circle of members and friends. Over the past two years, $16,000 in funded grants has been awarded to church members for REACH grant projects.

Brochures regarding First Unitarian's Endowment Fund may be found on the table in the church's foyer.

The Committee is grateful to the contributors to the Endowment Fund. While trying to be inclusive in this listing, we apologize if we have unintentionally omitted anyone's name.

Please feel free to contact any of the Endowment Fund Committee members:
I have chosen to omit all contact information for the individuals listed on the original document but this is where you would include a list of committee members and their contact information in your own document.

---

1   Reprinted by permission of the First Unitarian Church of Des Moines, Iowa

STATEMENT OF INTENT / INDIVIDUAL

TO MAKE A CASH OR DEFERRED GIFT TO ST. TIMOTHY'S CHURCH

As an indication of my support to St. Timothy's Church, I am pleased to indicate that it is my intention to provide a gift for the church as follows:

Type of gift (outright gift of cash or negotiable asset):

_____

Timing of the gift:_____During my lifetime, or, _____Deferred

With the understanding that values are subject to change, I estimate the current value of my gift to be approximately $_____.

Purpose of the gift:

_____I wish my gift to be unrestricted and may be used where the need of the church is greatest.

_____I direct my gift to be used for the following purpose(s):

_____

_____

My attorney:

_____
NAME OF FIRM

_____
FIRM ADDRESS

_____
CITY, STATE, ZIP

_____ has been informed of this statement.

SIGNATURE AND ADDRESS OF DONOR

_____The church may send a copy of this Statement of Intent to my attorney.

_____I will send a copy to my attorney.

_____   _____   _____
DONOR SIGNATURE   PRINT NAME   DATE

_____
ADDRESS

_____   _____   _____
CITY, STATE, ZIP   TELEPHONE

_____   _____   _____
ATTORNEY SIGNATURE   PRINT NAME   DATE

STATEMENT OF INTENT / COUPLE

TO MAKE A CASH OR DEFERRED GIFT TO ST. TIMOTHY'S CHURCH

As an indication of my support to St. Timothy's Church, we are pleased to indicate that it is our intention to provide a gift for the church or indicated herein:

Type of gift (outright gift of cash or negotiable asset), will trust or other:

_____

With the understanding that values are subject to change, We estimate the current value of our future gift to be approximately $_____.

Purpose of the gift:

_____We wish our gift to be unrestricted and may be used where the need of the church is greatest.

_____We wish to specify that our gift be used for the following purpose(s):

_____

_____

Our attorney(ies):

_____

NAME OF FIRM

_____

FIRM ADDRESS

_____

CITY, STATE, ZIP

_____has been informed of this statement.

SIGNATURE AND ADDRESS OF DONOR AND ATTORNEY

_____The church may send a copy of this Statement of Intent to my attorney.

_____I will send a copy to my attorney.

_____	_____	_____
DONOR SIGNATURE	PRINT NAME	DATE
_____	_____	_____
DONOR SIGNATURE	PRINT NAME	DATE

_____

ADDRESS

_____	_____
CITY, STATE, ZIP	TELEPHONE

_____	_____	_____
ATTORNEY SIGNATURE	PRINT NAME	DATE

BIBLIOGRAPHY

"Affluence and Altruism," *Philanthropy Matters,* Volume 15, Issue 1, The Center on Philanthropy, Indiana University, Indianapolis, IN, 2007

American Express Charitable Gift Survey, The Center on Philanthropy, Indiana University, Indianapolis, IN, November 2007

Bank of America Study of High Net-Work Philanthropy, The Center on Philanthropy, Indiana University, Indianapolis, IN, October 2006

Borg, Marcus J., *The Heart of Christianity,* Harper-Collins, New York, NY, 1995

Burlingame, Dwight F., *Altruism and Philanthropy,* The Center on Philanthropy, Indiana University, Indianapolis, IN, 1998

Callahan, Kennon L., *Effective Church Finances,* Jossey-Bass, San Francisco, CA, 1992

Callahan, Kennon L., *Giving and Stewardship in an Effective Church,* Jossey-Bass, San Francisco, CA, 1992

Clinton, Bill, *Giving: How Each of Us Can Change the World,* Alfred Knopf, New York, NY, 2007

Daloz, Laurent Parks*, Can Generosity Be Taught?,* The Center on Philanthropy, Indiana University, Indianapolis, IN, 1998

Danko, William D. and Stanley, Thomas J., *The Millionaire Next Door,* MJF Books, New York, NY, 1996

Eker, T. Harv, *Secrets of the Millionaire Mind,* Harper-Collins, New York, NY, 2005

Emerson, Michael O., Smith, Christian, and Snell, Patricia, *Passing the Plate,* Oxford University Press, New York, NY, 2008

Gardner, Howard, *Changing Minds: The Art and Science of Changing Our Own and Other People's Minds,* Harvard Business School Press, Boston, MA, 2004

"Giving Insights for Non-Profits," *Philanthropy Matters,* Volume 14, Issue 1, The Center on Philanthropy, Indiana University, Indianapolis, IN, 2006

Giving USA™ 2008, Giving USA Foundation™, Chicago, IL, 2008

Goleman, Daniel, *Emotional Intelligence,* Bantam Books, New York, NY, 1997

Green, Bill, *52 Ways to Ignite Your Congregation… Generous Giving,* Pilgrim Press, Cleveland, OH, 2010

Hogan, Kevin, *The Psychology of Persuasion,* Pelican Publishing Company, Gretna, LA, 2004

Jamieson, Janet T., and Jamieson, Philip D., *Ministry and Money: A Practical Guide For Pastors,* Westminister John Knox Press, Louisville, KY

Keltner, Dacher, *Born To Be Good,* Norton, W. W. & Company, Inc, New York and London, January 2009

Krauser, E., *Executive Summary: Bequest Giving Study for Campbell and Company,* The Center on Philanthropy, Indiana University, Indianapolis, IN, March 2007

Lawson, Douglas M., *Give to Live,* Alti Publishing, La Jolla, CA, 1991

Lawson, Douglas M., *More Give to Live,* Alti Publishing, La Jolla, CA, 2003

Needleman, Jacob, *Money and the Meaning of Life,* Doubleday, New York, NY, 1994

"The Revolving Door," *Philanthropy Matters,* Volume 16, Issue 1, The Center on Philanthropy, Indiana University, Indianapolis, IN, 2008

Schaller, Lyle E., *The New Context for Ministry,* Abingdon Press, Nashville, TN, 2002

Smith, Christian; Emerson, Michael O., and Snell, Patricia, *Passing the Plate,* Oxford University Press, Oxford, NY, 2008

Sharpe, Robert F., *Before You Give Another Dime,* Thomas Nelson Publishers, Nashville, TN, 1979

Tolle, Eckhart, *A New Earth, Awakening to Your Life's Purpose,* Penguin Group, New York, NY, USA, 2006

Tolle, Eckhart, *The Power of Now,* New World Library, Novato, CA, 1999

"Weathering an Uncertain Economy," *Philanthropy Matters,* Volume 16, Issue 2, The Center on Philanthropy, Indiana University, Indianapolis, IN, 2008

Witherington, Ben, *Jesus and Money,* Brazos Press, Grand Rapids, MI, 2010

Wuthnow, Robert, *Faith and Giving: From Christian Charity To Spirtual Practice,* The Center on Philanthropy, Indiana University, Indianapolis, IN, 2004

INDEX

21st century church must transform 35

A Biblical Pledge Program 16
A Complete Stewardship Program For Your Church 93
A Motivated Advocate 16
A Process of Local Church Vitalization 94, 95
A Program for Reversing Heart Disease 104
a relationship… with your congregants 4
a sense of appreciation, of gratitude 62
A strong interest in, or involvement with, a specific
        program 61
A System Approach to Stewardship 61, 67, 94, 95
Aaron Feuerstein 97, 98, 100
Abraham Maslow 58
accessorize with religion 12
act of spiritual commitment 22
additional factors… motivate people to give… 62
additional obstacles 21
Agreement with the goals and mission of the
        institution 61
Allen Luks 103
altruism and egoism 58
Altruism and Philanthropy 58, 67
Altruism is one end of a continuum 57
Alzheimer's victims 81
American Christians give away relatively little money 46
American Institute of Motivation Research 57, 58, 73
An Experiment in District Revitalization 93
Another remedy for fear of asking for money 21
Anticipate questions and objections 74
anxiety 72, 102
appeal to generosity 101
appeal to people's highest nature 101
appeal to the prospect's emotions 74
appointment at their home is the safest 78
appreciation and heartfelt thanks 26, 104
as spiritual as baptizing a baby 7
Ask for gifts 38, 66, 78
ask us to help you develop the concept 30
Assuage of guilt feelings 59
Assure your clients that your meeting… will be kept in
        strict confidence 80
Atlanta, Georgia 8
attempt to fill their spiritual void 29
attitudes toward money 5, 7, 22, 26, 27
authority to confer worth 10

baby boomers i, 2, 4, 24, 64
baby boomers have different attitudes 2
bankers 49, 86
Bank of America 63, 64, 65, 67, 68, 78
Barack Obama 70, 71
Barron's 86
be absolutely transparent 66
be clear about the goals and mission of the organization 63
becoming a role model 36, 73
behavior is not understandable 69, 73
being asked 63, 65, 78
being involved in the Church as an adult 61
benefits the donors will derive 77
benefits to the Donors Paragraph 84
Benjamin Franklin 8
be proactive in including businesspeople 30
bequeather 63, 64, 86
Bequest Giving Study for Campbell and Company 64, 68
bequests by will to charities in 2006 64
biblical base 15
biggest obstacle to involvement: the lack of education
        in stewardship and money 21
Bill and Melinda Gates 60, 99
Bill Clinton 70
Billy Graham 70
Bishop Gerald Ensley 34
Bishop Palmer 36
Bishop Ruben Job Center for Learning Development 93
Blue Ribbon Weekend 38
Born To Be Good 58, 67
Boy Scout 48
bring about a desired impact 63, 64, 65
budget i, 2, 11, 27, 43, 45, 69, 71, 78, 84
business men and women 49
but where no plan is laid 85
by making a will 54

calendar year 2001 45
call and make an appointment 78
campaign to upgrade and expand the camp and retreat
        sites 3
capacity of ordinary American Christians to transform
        the world 43
capacity to foster massive and unprecedented spiritual,
        social, cultural, and economic change 43
capital campaign ii, 12, 23, 25, 38, 47, 88
Carl Diederichs 94

Carl Rogers 58
Celebrity Fundraiser 17
Center for Parish Development 61, 67, 93–95
Center on Philanthropy at Indiana University ii, 1, 2,
        37, 87, 93, 107
Center on Wealth and Philanthropy at Boston College 4
certified public accountants 86
challenge i, 1, 4, 8, 12, 13, 16, 22, 25, 30, 31, 33, 35–37,
        39, 42, 61, 77, 87, 92, 103
    of determining who has wealth and the task of
        establishing a relationship 36
    to give 16
    to recognize 30
characteristics of millionaires 44, 45
charismatic evangelist 8
Charitable 54
    bequests 4, 54
    gift in their will 65
    gift plans and mechanisms 4
Charles O'Malley 53
checkbook 9
choose your seating arrangement to your advantage 79
Christian Gospels 58
Christians 7, 9, 29, 43, 46, 92, 93
    are responsible 7
    doing financial planning 93
    in the United States earned a total collective
        income in 2005 in the trillions of dollars 43
Christians Doing Financial Planning 93
Christian support groups 30
Christina Hixson 100
church membership or association with the institution 61
church was afraid of their entrepreneurial instincts 30
Clarence Tompkins 9, 10, 81
clear policies 21
clergy i, 1–4, 7, 8, 10, 19–23, 25, 27–31, 33, 35, 38,
        41–43, 57, 58, 61, 70, 79, 93, 99, 101
clergyperson 29, 57
clients served 16
College of Agriculture 38, 46
College of Family and Consumer Science 46
College of Home Economics 46
Columbia, South Carolina 15, 37, 93
communication plan 86
competition for the charitable dollar i, 2, 24, 25, 33
Conference i, ii, 1–4, 8, 15, 19, 21, 22, 25, 33–37, 40,
        61, 81, 82, 91, 93
    Minister ii, 1, 2, 8, 21, 25, 33, 34, 35, 36
    ministers and their boards 34
    systems 34

confidence 4, 17, 21, 62, 80
confidential information 49
conflict of interest 10
conscious level 59, 72
consensus 17
contemporary American Christians 46
contribute to the spiritual life of our children, youth,
        adults, and families 13
Creating Congregational Cultures of Generosity 93
Crown Financial Ministers 92
cultivating wealthy parishioners 3
cultivation of prospective donors 29

Dacher Keltner 58, 67
Daniel Hudson Burnham 85
Dave Ramsey organization 92
deep ambivalence in the system 34
deepening and centering in God 19, 29
deeply spiritual, transformational process 28
deferred gift i, 19, 20, 25, 27, 28, 36, 38, 39, 42, 43, 45,
        46, 53, 54, 55, 57, 64, 66, 74, 81, 85–87, 91
defines wealth as the current value of ones assets, less
        liabilities 44
degrees of frustration 7
demands on their time and energies 23
demonstrating the commitment of others 17
denominational executives ii, 2, 4, 33, 35–39
denominations are not providing support 21
describe the need 77, 83
desire and Ability 16
desire to engage in developing 30
desire to participate 16
Des Moines, Iowa 10, 26, 28, 31, 55, 57, 71, 86, 92,
        108, 109
develop a list of twenty-five of your parishioners who
        have wealth 37
develop a quality relationship 27
develop a three-to five-year plan for the finance
        committee and/or the deferred gift committee 85
Developing Financial Stewardship, A Resource for
        Cultivating Christian Stewardship for use with
        Church Leaders 94
devout households 65
dialogue with the Executive Director of the
        denomination 30
differences in characteristics 64
Director of Denominational Advancement for the
        Christian Reformed Church 30
dissemination of best practices 35
District Council on Ministries 94
distrust large organizations 24

do their part 45

donor 2, 4, 12, 14, 24, 27, 29, 38, 42, 45, 47, 48, 54, 55,
57, 58, 59, 60, 62, 63, 64, 65, 66, 71, 72, 77, 78,
81, 82, 83, 84, 87, 100, 103
linkage (connection, relating) 16
motivation 57, 62

donors… interested in the results of their giving 24

don't attempt to assume leadership for a capital
campaign in your own parish 88

don't take a turn-down personally 81

Dr. Clarice Auluck-Wilson 99

Dr. Dean Ornish 102, 104

Dr. Douglas M. Lawson 7, 26, 30, 93, 97, 100, 102, 103,
104, 105, 107

Dr. Hans Selye 103

Dr. Herbert Benson 102

Dr. James Lynch 104

Dr. John Thomas 23

Dr. Marcus Borg 19, 28, 31

Dr. Martin Jischke 36, 38

Dr. Norman Vincent Peale 70, 102

Dr. Paul Dietterich 19, 67, 93–95, 107

Dr. Peter Harkema 30, 31

Dr. Phil 12

Dr. Wesley A. Rediger 15

dream of a health center 81

Dwight Burlingame 57, 58, 67, 107

Dwight Heinrichs 53

eagle feather given by a five-year-old 100

earliest attitudes toward money 26

early Methodist movement 8

economic recession of 2008–11 42

educate yourself to do major gift solicitation 28

educating yourself about money 85

efforts to increase giving may appear to be self-serving 22

effort to get UCC leaders 1, 8, 34

ego-gratification 59

elderly, wealthy people 36

emotional 17, 29, 57, 59, 66, 72, 73, 74, 100, 102, 103, 104
and irrational causes 57, 59
physical and spiritual benefits of altruism 29, 66,
100, 103
security 59

emotions or feeling experiences 73

Emphasize the religious and biblical teachings about
giving 66

emphasizing
generosity 3, 101
generosity and lifting up the qualities of generous
people 101

encourage your people to make a will 55

encouraging the pastors to become involved in the
process 36

essential and legitimate role of denominational
leaders 35

essential part of the life of discipleship 11

Establishing solid relationships takes time 37

establish trusts 47

Estate planning attorneys 86

ever-increasing competition for the charitable
dollar 24

every day of our lives you and I are the benefactors of
the generosity of others 99

everything to gain 73

Every Transaction is Powered by God 17

excellent
candidate to present a case 28
communication skills 27
plan that addresses the roles and responsibilities of
denominational leadership 34

Executive Director of the Center for Parish
Development 93

expectation that they will bankroll projects 30

Explain the solution 77

extensive study on motivation for giving to the
Church 58

fails to recognize 25

Failure to minister and relate to businesspeople 30

Faith and Fundraising 15, 37, 93

farm 4, 9, 41, 45, 47, 48, 49, 82
economy has changed dramatically 45
families are in a special category 45
land valued in the millions 4
managers 49

"father of stress reduction" 103

fear
of failure 21
of project failure 17
of rejection 21

fears, frustrations, hopes and dreams 73

feedback that indicates the results of the gifts 66

feel about wealth in general, and about wealthy
people 27

feelings 7, 30, 59, 60, 72, 103

feelings of helplessness, annoyance, and aversion to the
issue [stewardship] 7

feeling valued 73

few concrete, obvious, and reliable indicators 25

fierce competition for money 2

finances as 'unspiritual' 7, 20

financial
>advisors 49, 81, 82, 86, 87, 92
>challenges 33
>circumstances of your family 26
>efforts will help all of the churches accomplish their financial goals 37
>planners 86
>secretary or treasurer 26
>support of God's work 11

Financial Accountability 17

Financial Equity within the Body of Christ 16

Financial Peace University 92

First Century Development Officers 17

First Unitarian Church in Des Moines, Iowa 55, 86, 108, 109

five steps to effective persuasion 74, 77

Flow: The Psychology of Peak Experience 102

focusing on the needs of donors 12

former Bishop of the Iowa Conference of the United Methodist Church 34

former Conference Minister of the Indiana-Kentucky Conference 8

Fort Dodge, Iowa 9, 13, 81

Francis Quarles 99

"friend-raising" 27

Friendship Haven 9, 13, 81

from a Report of a study conducted by the United Church of Christ 33

fulfilling life 11

fundraiser was out of touch with feminist reality 80

fundraising i, ii, 1–5, 7–15, 19–23, 24, 25, 27, 29, 33–40, 43, 63, 66, 71, 81, 85–87, 89, 91, 93, 95

fundraising for them is ministry 22

future of giving looks bright 4

gathering and recording information 28, 86

General Minister of the United Church of Christ (UCC) 23

generosity 3, 5, 11, 12, 23, 28, 29, 42, 60, 62, 66, 72, 73, 92, 93, 97, 99, 100–105
>brings about personal physical, emotional, and spiritual benefits 66
>Can Generosity Be Taught? 97, 105
>is a response 102
>ranks among the highest, most noble-minded 100

generous
>people enjoy many physical and emotional and spiritual benefits 100
>people often enjoy a sense of satisfaction that by joining with others 100
>with time, knowledge, energy, and influence 99

George Whitfield 8

getting a message across is a good thing 12

get your hands on lists of donors to other projects or capital campaigns 47

give God some time 81

Give to Live and More Give to Live 102

Give to Live, How Giving Can Change Your Life 93

giving ii, 1, 2, 4, 5, 7–9, 12, 16–27, 29, 30, 34, 37, 38, 43, 45, 47, 50, 54, 55, 57, 58, 59–68, 73, 87, 91, 93, 94, 97, 98, 100–104, 107
>back to society 63, 64, 65
>from duty certainly has its limitations 12
>is not to be discussed 20
>produces friendship 18
>produces glory 18
>produces prayer 18
>produces resources 17
>produces results 18
>produces testimonials to the Cross 18
>produces thanks 17
>records 26

Giving Above and Beyond 16

"Giving and sharing not only help others, they also give us life." 97

Giving and Stewardship in an Effective Church 65, 68

Giving USATM 2008 54, 55, 64, 68

good
>clues as to how to identify wealth 44
>deed 103, 104

goodness of God 104

Good Samaritan 7

Goodwill Industries 99

Gospel of Jesus Christ 11

Grace: The Ultimate Gift 18

Great Depression of the 1930s 42, 45

greatest single change in church finances 45

greed squeezes out values 11

guidance regarding the needs of the church 28

hands-on, experimental research 98

Harold E. Hughes 53, 91

Harry Stout 8

Healthy Pleasures 30, 103

heartened by all of the discussion 12

'helper's high' 103

help those with less 64, 65

"He who gives all, though but little, gives much…" 99

hidden emotional reasons 73

high-net-worth
>donors rely on fundraisers 87
>"high net-worth" households 63, 64, 65, 74

history of generous giving to the church 30

honorable sense of responsibility 101

honoring God 9
household income greater than $200,000 63
how
    I see the practice of fundraising as advocated in
        this book 23
    this program is unique 77
    to identify the millionaires 42
huge transfer of wealth from the 'boomers to their
    children 4
Hugh Blair (1822) 85
human behavior is not understandable in ordinary
    common sense terms 69, 73
Humanize individuals and groups 66
human nature 58

"I have a responsibility… " 98
identification of wealthy members 29
identified dozens of millionaires 4
idolatry 10
if committed Christians… in the United States gave 10
    percent of their after-tax-income 46
"If I know who is giving… " 25
If they give consent, announce their commitment 81
If they seem to hesitate, ask what concerns them 80
"If you die without making a will, you'll never do it
    again." 53
II Corinthians 8:1 15
II Corinthians 8:2 15
II Corinthians 8:3 16
II Corinthians 8:4 16
II Corinthians 8:5 16
II Corinthians 8:6 16
II Corinthians 8:7 16
II Corinthians 8:8 16
II Corinthians 8:9 16
II Corinthians 8:10 16
II Corinthians 8:11 16
II Corinthians 8:12 16
II Corinthians 8:13–15 16
II Corinthians 8:16–17 16
II Corinthians 8:18 17
II Corinthians 8:19 15, 17
II Corinthians 8:19–20 17
II Corinthians 8:22 17
II Corinthians 8:23–24 17
II Corinthians 9:2 17
II Corinthians 9:3 17
II Corinthians 9:6 17
II Corinthians 9:7 17
II Corinthians 9:10 17
II Corinthians 9:11 17

II Corinthians 9:12 15, 18
II Corinthians 9:13 18
II Corinthians 9:14 18
II Corinthians Chapters Eight and Nine 8
image of a generous God 11
"I'm not very good with money because I'm not very
    good with money myself." 21
important aspect of ministry 20
impoverishment of sensuality 26, 104
"…improving the system of internal communication…" 87
in a position to influence hundreds of pastors and
    church leaders 33
In most cases your prospective donors know you well 27
"In the new ecclesiastical economy, credibility is
    increasingly performance-based… " 87
Inagrace Dietterich 19, 67, 93–95, 107
income is not linked with their performance 22
increase giving 22, 66
increasing skills of persuasion 3
Indiana University ii, 2, 5, 8, 34, 37, 40, 64, 67, 68, 87,
    93, 105, 107
indicates that you have done your homework 78
indictment against the 'choosing not to know since I
    might show favoritism' 25
individuals 4, 11, 21, 24, 30, 37, 38, 47–49, 60, 64–66,
    72, 73, 82, 84, 87, 92
influence of fear 21
influence of the emotions 58
inform ourselves 29
infusion of bequests 4
Inside the envelope was a single feather 97
insurance executives 49
Intellectual Giving vs. Emotional Giving 17
interests, values and involvement 74
interviews with many clergy 29
Introductory Paragraph 83
Investors Business Daily 86
Involve as many of your wealthy members as possible 66
Involvement in a capital campaign to raise funds for a
    specific program 62
Iowa Conference i, ii, 3, 4, 22, 25, 34, 61, 81, 82, 91
Iowa State University i, 3, 36, 38, 46, 62, 71, 100

Jacob Needleman 92
James Andreoni 57, 58
Janet and Philip Jamieson 29, 31
Jesus 7, 11, 12, 15, 16, 97, 99, 101
Jimmy LaRose 15
Job descriptions 35
Jo Childs 100
John J. Havens 4

John Kennedy 70

John Wesley 9, 15, 70

joining a great company of noble and generous people 101

keep

the costs of administration, including fundraising, at a minimum 66

your eyes and ears open to the existence of family and community trusts 87

your research and records highly confidential 47

keeps the congregation informed about what the Church is doing 87

Kennon Callahan 65, 68

Kevin Hogan 69, 70, 72, 73, 75, 107

key

question 57

relationship between cost and joy in discipleship 11

Kiplinger Letter 86

Kiplinger's 86

lack of support

from their churches 29

from their superiors 21

Lake Institute on Faith and Giving at Indiana University 34

large congregations 49

largest segment of society today 24

Larry Burkett 92

Laura Nash and Scotty McLennan 29, 31

Laurence Daloz 97, 105

"Law of Association" 71

"Law of Conformity" 71

"Law of Consistency" 71

"Law of Contrast" 71

"Law of Expectancy" 71

"Law of Friends" 71

"Law of Power" 72

"Law of Reciprocity" 70

"Law of Scarcity" 71

lawyers 49, 53, 87

leaders 3, 8

in education, politics, business, commerce, and religion 70

of denominations can 33, 35

learning to grow in generosity 11

Legacy Society 108

lifestyle 10, 11

Lift up

causes 66

critical needs 66

little awareness of or interest in denominational ministries 34

Live-the-Vision 9

local church 1, 2, 8, 11, 24, 30, 34, 35, 61, 94, 95

Local Farm Bureau or County Extension Office 48

loneliness 59, 60, 72, 103, 104

long-range plan 85

Los Angeles, California 2, 58, 67, 75

love God with all our heart 11

Love objects 60

loving our neighbors as we love ourselves 58

Lyle Schaller 2, 5, 33, 40, 43, 45–47, 51, 87, 88, 107

Macedonia 8, 15

Make no little plans 85

makes everyone… richer 104

making a case for generosity 12

Malcolm Forbes (1977) 53

Malden Mills 97

manufacturer's Christmas paychecks 100

many

clergy like me, grew up in low or lower-middle class families 21

farm families are generous with their time and energy 45

opportunities to harvest major and deferred gifts 27

reasons why people decline to make a specific gift 81

wealthy couples and individuals 4

Mark Twain 41

Martin Jischke 36, 38

Martin Luther King, Jr. 70

McDonalds 48

means of helping others 8

Meet critical needs 63, 65

member's or couple's attitudes 25

message heard by working and businesspeople 29

Methodist minister 34, 81

methods of promoting giving 29

ministers' attitudes toward money 22

minister's role 11

Ministry and Money: A Practical Guide For Pastors 29, 31

mitzvah 104

Money i, 1, 2, 5, 7–11, 20–23, 26–28, 29, 31, 37, 38, 42, 43, 46, 48, 54, 57, 61, 63, 65, 70, 71, 77, 84–86, 92, 99, 103

claims the place of God 10

management of your congregants 92

Money and the Meaning of Life 92

Moravian Ministry Foundation in America 94

more effective and more valuable leader 28

More Give to Live 102, 104, 105

more than half of adults polled do not have a will 54
more wealthy people in the U.S. today 24
Morningside College i, 3, 41, 81
Moses 70
most people
    ... generate their own salaries 22
    want and need recognition 26
most transparent theological document 11
move to the case, the story 79
must make the issue a priority 23

Narcissism 60
National Development Institute in Columbia, South
    Carolina 93
natural for raising money 27
need for training for pastors 35
Needs Paragraph 83
need to rethink board structure and membership 34
negative attitudes toward business and
    businesspeople 29
neighbor 11, 58, 71, 102, 104
new culture 2, 23, 33, 34
new set of skills 28
no commissions, no bonuses for performance 22
no experience with wealthy people 21
non-profit charitable organizations in the United States 2
Nonprofits
    need to prepare 4
    should provide services when government
        can't 63, 65
Norman Vincent Peale 70, 102
nothing mysterious or magical about engaging in
    stewardship 21
not suggesting that you devote a lot of time to major
    gift work 28
Now, present the proposal 79
number of family foundations increased 47

October of 2007 15, 105
Old and New Testaments 7, 101
old model 12
one of the last modern taboos: soliciting donations 1, 8, 34
one-to-one fundraising practice has "come of age" 24
on-going process 86
opportunities to cultivate wealthy parishioners 5
optimism 12
ordinary American Christians as a group are sitting on
    utterly enormous monetary resources 43
Organize a "Heritage Circle" or "Future Society" 86
orphanage 8
other people will respect you 73

ownership of farm land 47
Oxford English Dictionary 57, 67

parents' attitudes toward money 26
part of building the kingdom of God 9
Passing the Plate 13, 20, 30, 43, 46, 51
pastor
    is the key to generating those resources 4
    needs to participate fully in all aspects of planning
        and promoting a campaign 12
    priest or rabbi 7, 27, 29, 57, 66
pastors
    need for training 35
Pastor's Resource Booklet 94
Patrick Rooney 2–5, 107
patterns of consumption 10
Paul G. Schervish 4
Paul's and Titus' fundraising 8
people 19, 24
    are, in general, more sophisticated 24
    are well aware of the pressing needs 24
    attempt to avoid pain 72
people's giving as a kind of spiritual thermometer 27
perpetual drumbeat of consumerism 10
Perry, Iowa 53
personal finances 27
persuasion 3, 5, 26–28, 69–71, 73–75, 77
philanthropic contributions to churches 34
Philanthropic Priorities 16
philanthropist in Las Vegas 100
Philanthropy ii, 2, 4, 5, 7, 13, 15, 24, 37, 40, 46, 57, 58,
    63, 64, 67, 68, 87, 93, 104, 105, 107
    "Philanthropy is the mystical mingling of a
        joyful giver, an artful asker, and a grateful
        recipient." 7
piece of the worship 9
plan for a series of seminars on estate planning 86
Plymouth Congregational Church 10, 57
pooling my gifts 101
population of older people... increasing
    exponentially 24
population of over-sixty-five 46
possessions 7, 9, 10, 12
Posturing the Team 17
post-World War II decades 45
potential
    for deferred gifts is to the Church 53
    for denominational executives 33, 35
    for major and deferred gifts 4, 25, 33, 35, 39, 42,
        43, 45, 46, 53, 54, 64, 65, 83, 91, 92
powerful preacher 8

preconscious 59, 72

preconscious level 72

preoccupation 10

Prepare a Compelling Proposal 77

Prepare yourself for the call 78

Preparing For and Making a Successful Call 74, 77, 79, 81, 83

President and Patty Jischke 36, 38

President George W. Bush 73

prime prospects 45, 46, 47, 65

private investors 48

process of cultivating and developing a relationship of
    trust and respect 27

process of transformation 29

Product/service helps many people just like you get
    that result 73

professional
    fundraisers 3, 15, 20, 23, 27, 86, 94, 102
    fundraising i, 1, 3, 4, 13, 15, 23, 81
    fundraising procedures 23

professionalism 25

Professor Mihaly Csikszentmihalyi 102

programs i, 1, 2, 4, 8, 12, 13, 20, 24, 34, 35, 57, 61, 62,
    83, 91, 99

Proof of Love 16

Proportionate giving 101

proposal 3, 14, 21, 27, 72, 74, 77, 78, 79, 80, 83, 84
    should be brief 78
    signed by two heavy hitters 77

PROPOSAL GUIDE 77, 83

PROSPECT INFORMATION FORM 37, 50, 86

prospect research 36

prospects for a planned gift 65

provide leadership in fundraising for their pastors 35

provide the donor(s) a copy of the signed Statement of
    Intent 81

Psychological Behavior 72

Psychology Today 102

public information 47, 49, 87

Publicity Announcing the Philanthropy of Others 15

Purdue University 36

pure altruism 57

purpose of the meeting 30

put in writing a three to five year plan for yourself 85

qualities of different candidates 28

raising funds… is as spiritual as praying, preaching, or
    serving communion 28

Recent scandals of some religious and political
    leaders 24

recognition 26, 59, 60, 98, 100, 101, 108

reflection of your spiritual life 9

refusing to use the power that could be used 20

Regard for the local church 61

"Relationship, relationship, relationship" 37

"… relationship with God that transforms us… " 19

relationship with God that transforms us 19, 29

relationship with our stuff 10

religion as a means of ultimate transformation 28

Religious beliefs 63, 64, 65

Religious beliefs were ranked highest among their [the
    devout's] reasons for giving 65

remind your prospects that the Building Committee
    proposed the project 80

Report of American Institute of Motivational
    Research 69

Request For Funds 84

research
    into motivation for giving 63
    thesis project 98

respect 97
    for the pastor/priest and other professional leaders 61
    for the volunteer leadership of the church or
      synagogue 61

Rev. Don Arthur 94

Rev. Doug Peters 26

Rev. Dr. Clarence Tompkins 9, 10, 81

Rev. Dr. David Ruhe 7, 10, 28, 107

Rev. Dr. Douglas M. Lawson 7, 26, 30, 93, 97, 100,
    102–105, 107

Rev. Dr. Larry Sonner 22

Rev. Dr. Rich Pleva 25, 107

Rev. Dr. Wayne Barrett 93

Rev. Janet Long 19

Rev. Jim Dotson 94

Rev. John H. Thomas 33, 34

Rev. Stephen Gray 1, 2, 8, 34, 35, 107

Rich Young Ruler 11

Robert Fogel 58

Ronald Reagan 70

Sadam Hussein 73

Sales people envision themselves closing the sale 79

scout camp 48

search/nominating committees 35

"Second Mile Committee" 86

secular
    agencies 33
    fundraising 22, 23

Seeking Pleasure — Avoiding Pain 72

see yourself doing a great job of presenting the case 79

self-awareness 25

self-creating autonomous engines of consumption 10

Self-interest 57, 58

self-preservation 59

seminars 2, 3, 34, 37, 66, 85–87, 92–94

seminars on faith and fundraising 37

seminary education did not include fundraising 3

Senior Pastor of Walnut Hills United Methodist
        Church in Des Moines 26

sense of gratitude 101

September 11, 2001 91

"share the dream" 80

Shell Rock congregation 94

should be careful to differentiate 30

Should you take another person with you on the call? 80

sincere comment or compliment 79

skills of persuasion 3, 5, 69, 70

Smith, Emerson, and Snell 20, 21, 30

Smith, Emerson, and Snell study 20, 21

Social acceptance 60

social, economic, attitudinal and population changes 33

society 63, 65

solicitation

        calls 12

        donations 1, 8, 34

Solution Paragraph 83

some parishioners consider the minister to be an
        "employee" 22

some wealthy parishioners occupy top positions in
        business, industry 36

Speaking the truth in love... 7, 12

spearheading an effort 1, 8, 34

Special Gifts Committee 86

spend yourself out of debt 92, 95

spirit-filled activities 7

spiritual

        growth 27, 29, 104

        health 25, 104

        process 9

spiritual to the core of their being 100, 104

Statement of Intent 81, 82

STATEMENT OF INTENT / COUPLE 111

STATEMENT OF INTENT / INDIVIDUAL 110

statements of several pastors 8

State Why You are Appealing To Them 83

Status seeking 60

Steps to Successful Major Gift Fundraising 14

stewardship

        and fundraising are spiritual 7, 21, 29

        and fundraising are 'unspiritual' 7

        Education for the Future 92

        expectations 21

Stewards of God's Gifts, A Resource for Studying the
        Biblical Understanding of Stewardship 94

Stewards of the Household of God 94

stock brokers 49

story is told in Mark 11

St. Patrick's Catholic Church 53

St. Paul's Theological Seminary in Kansas City 80

strong, rational and emotional case 74

study of philanthropy 63

successful fundraisers ask for gifts of a specific amount 78

survey commissioned by The Non-Profit Times 54

symptom of a deeper spiritual problem 19

system has very limited experience 34

Tailor the proposal 77

tax advisors 86

tax return 11

teachings of Jesus 7, 101

Tecumseh, Michigan 102

ten-year study of 2,700 men 102

testing the water 81

textile mill in Lawrence, Massachusetts 97

Thank the prospects 77

thank you 13, 79, 81, 84

the ability to monitor their behavior 25

The Apostle Paul 8, 15, 17, 23, 70, 101

The ask 3, 78

the bequeathers 63, 64

The Bible 7, 70

The Board of Discipleship of the United Methodist
        Church 93

The Broken Heart — The Medical Consequences of
        Loneliness 104

The Call Back 80

The Center for Parish Development in Chicago 61, 93

the desire to be identified with others who are
        supporting a program or organization 62

the devout 63, 65

The Essence of a Major Donor Ministry 15

THE HERITAGE CIRCLE 86, 89

The Impoverished Donor 15

the joy of generating gifts for your cause, your church 82

The Joy of Receiving the Check 82

the Millionaire Next Door 41, 44, 51

The needs for support of local church programs and
        ministries are staggering 24

the need to do good for one another and the need to
        love and respect one another 97

The New Context for Ministry 5, 33, 40, 51, 88

The new face of American philanthropy 2

The Physical, Psychological, and Spiritual Benefits of Altruism 102

The Psychology of Persuasion 70, 75

the rationale, "don't want to know" 25

There's a new culture around how we fund missions and ministry 33

The Stewardship Academy 93

the strategy of ownership 72

the "taboo" about discussing giving 20

The Ultimate Gift 16, 18

the use of contributions as instruments of power 62

the very wealthy 53, 63

The Wall Street Journal 86

they contributed "because they were asked" 78

think about employing a full or part-time person to do major 86

this is not a "social call" 79

This is what I hope to accomplish 85

This product/service is guaranteed 73

those who

decide to make planned gifts 54

have chosen service careers 99

have much have an obligation to help 66

three-and four-day seminars on fundraising 34

thriving retirement home 9

tithe sets the bar of responsibility much lower for the wealthy 101

Tithing 24, 101

tithing is a rigid and legalistic concept 101

to be effective 23, 29

Today's generation of mature adults 45

to increase the level of giving beyond the duration of the current capital campaign 23

top prospective donors 12

Torah 58, 104

traditional modes of financing ministries... have diminished 24

tragic result 29, 42

training opportunities 35

transformation of the thinking 19

tremendous potential for raising millions of dollars 43

trillion-dollar transfer i, 4, 24, 25, 39, 54

trying to speak the truth in love 11

Try it once 73

TV evangelists 70

twenty successful businesspeople 30

typical village in India 98

UCC ii, 1, 2, 8, 10, 23, 24, 25, 33, 34, 35, 39, 40, 86, 107

has recognized the problems of funding ministry 34

Indiana-Kentucky Conference 1, 8, 34

leaders 1, 8, 34

unconscious or subconscious 59, 72

Uniqueness Paragraph 84

United Church News 5, 13, 30, 34, 40

United Church of Christ (UCC) ii, 1, 2, 8, 10, 23, 24, 25, 33, 34, 35, 39, 40, 86, 107

United Methodist Foundation of Michigan 93

United States 2, 8, 27, 43, 45, 46, 54, 63, 64, 73, 98

University of Maryland School of Medicine 104

university presidents 36

untapped wealth in the churches 4

updated, correct method of funding 35

up-side potential for good in U.S. Christian giving is immense 43

value of gratitude, of appreciation 66

very effective fundraiser 8

very wealthy were more concerned... about their ability to determine the impact of their gifts 63

Vicki Dischner 98

view of money and giving as an essential part of faithful, daily Christian living 8

Volunteer Advocacy 17

Volunteering 3, 61, 103

volunteer skills in non-profits 63, 65

'warm glow' of philanthropy 57

Washington Avenue Christian Church (Disciples) 19

Waterloo District of the United Methodist Church in Iowa 93

ways to recognize individuals 66

WealthEngine 49

wealthy people 19–22, 24, 27, 29, 36, 37, 42, 47, 49, 78

well-thought-out plan 74

we matter to someone 26, 104

we should give the concept of generosity... the place of value and high honor that it deserves 101

What Can Be Done to Help Women in a Typical Village Help Themselves? 98

what motivates

church people to give 58

people to give 57, 102

Whatsoever a Man Soweth that Shall He Also Reap 17

who is giving what to your parish, church 27

who is really at the center of the universe 11

Who makes a will? 54

why you are appealing to him/her 77

widening gap between the "haves" and the "have nots" 24

widow's penny 100

Winston Churchill 70

woman
    funding scholarships for thousands of
        disadvantaged students 100
    providing a high school for girls in a village in
        India 100
    providing little baby caskets 100
Women's Circle 98
workshops for clergy and church leaders 8
would give more if they were 'able to use their skills in
    non-profits' 65
written guidelines 35

you are not ready to make a formal proposal 80
You can do, have, or be more and feel better 73
You can reach your dreams 73
you may be the key 25, 82
"You need a plan. You can't start this journey without
    knowin' where you're goin.'" 85
you need to have a pledge card ready 79
you really just want to share the need with your
    prospect(s) 80
young man was possessed by his possessions 12
"Younger Americans are far more likely… to challenge
    the credibility of corporations…" 87